The Coming of the White Stag

Andrew Fry

To Jonathan and Olga

PROFILE

Andrew was born in Torquay in 1961. Although, he has spent most of his life in Barnstaple, North Devon. He had a normal education, although, he was born with Cerebral Palsy. Andrew has worked in two Factories, one Shop, the Barnstaple town library and also been a volunteer in the town Museum for a time, between this he has travelled widely as well as being a local counsellor.

Over the years Andrew has campaigned in N. Devon for the Labour Party. Writing as he has done also for several Magazines and two or three Newspapers. In the early nineties he also wrote a Play for the 'Chicken Shed', a Disabled Theatre Company. In twenty ten he took part in Barnstaple's Theatre Fest that happens in June. Since this he also was asked to take part in not one, but two Appledore Book Festivals, having been on local Radio.

During the summer of 1988, Andrew was awarded a Bursary to attend Toteigh Barton, a Writer's Retreat. Here he was Tutored by John

Moat, John Fairfax, and Ted Hughes. It was after this that he began writing and publishing his Poetry. Amazon and some limited Waterstone's outlets in the Home Counties stock his books.

CONTENTS

p.15 The Coming of the White Stag
p.16 Boudica
p.17 Virginal Heart
p.18 Carolling as One with the Trinity
p.20 The Universal Garden
p.22 The Rainbow
p.23 The Acorn and the Jay Bird
p.25 Raven Bird
p.26 At the Home of the Red Shoe
p.27 Smoke and Mirrors
p.28 Shakespeare in the Bible of Care
p.29 The Phoenix
p.31 Miracle on Boutport Street
p.32 A Quaker's View
p.33 Old Jim
p.34 Cockermouth Queen
p.36 The Lightning Seed
p.37 Old Cottonoplis
p.39 Public Rant, Society Needs to Change, Not I
p.40 Musing on the Standing Stones
p.41 Lake Land
p.42 Pilgrimage
p.43 Let Go!
p.44 Harvest Festival Fare at the Nicholls

p.46 In the Dark Town
p.48 Ignorants
p.49 The Future
p.50 Instow
p.52 The Journey
p.54 Walking the Old Line
p.56 Sea Gulls
p.57 The Jarrow Crusade
p.59 Fairy Steeling
p.60 Not Completing
p.61 Wings of Dinosaurs
p.62 Southport
p.63 I am
p.64 Barrow Rock
p.65 Voyage
p.66 Kites
p.67 Dorothy's Garden
p.69 Women
p.70 Looking Glass
p.71 Cataract
p.72 Social Media
p.73 The Dragon Awakens
p.75 The Kremlin's Cabal
p.76 Four Horsemen
p.77 Michael
p.78 Birthday Wishes

p.79　Get Inked
p.80　Teddy
p.81　First Footing
p.82　The Orphan
p.83　When the Moon and the Tide come up to say Goodbye
p.85　Fish Tides and the Sea Weed
p.86　Glossop Ward
p.88　In the Waiting Room
p.90　I'm a Poet
p.91　Turned
p.92　TV
p.93　Have you seen the Magical Colours in the Rain?
p.94　Puck
p.96　Julian
p.97　White Feather
p.98　Dark Water
p.99　The Sea
p.100　To the Queen of Crime Fiction
p.101　My Creed
p.103　The Statue
p.104　Autumn has Arrived
p.105　Black Boys in the Dark
p.107　The Cathedral
p.108　Flavour

p.109 I Give
p.110 Flatland-Fenland
p.111 Be a Broadcaster
p.112 Does Anyone have a Green Heart?
p.113 Phone Call from my Friend
p.115 Windows on the World
p.116 Rough Water
p.117 In this the Beautiful House of Bailey
p.118 Lee Abbey
p.119 Oh Blessed are the Poor
p.120 Something is Wrong Minister
p.121 Silver River Rain
p.122 Golden Brown
p.123 The Last Dregs of Summer
p.124 Poetry in the Rain
p.125 The Water of Life
p.126 Solstice Poem
p.127 Winter has Settled Now
p.128 The Yellow Star
p.129 The Dreamless Sleep
p.130 The Lost Generation
p.131 Shadow on my Mind
p.132 Oh Please Remember
p.133 Moving On
p.134 Sodom and Gomorrah Comes to Town
p.135 Mary's Poem

p.136 Destiny's Dream
p.138 She Who Weeps for Me
p.139 Long Time Coming
p.140 Abortion
p.141 Alcohol
p.143 Smoking in Bed
p.144 Have You Read Me?
p.146 It's Another Day
p.147 With Me!
p.148 Hartland Quay
p.149 Ghost Bears
p.152 It's That Cheeky Bear Poem
p.154 She's a Waldorf Super Star
p.156 The Glastonbury Call
p.157 Observation Poem
p.158 The Ole Silver Fox and His Story
p.160 The Griffins Tale
p.162 The Silent Island Acorn Tree
p.164 The Pilgrim, Saint, and the Unicorn's Horn
p.165 The Peregrine
p.167 Resume
p.168 The Gift
p.169 A Most Joyful of Pilgrims
p.172 Children of Jerusalem
p.174 Conflict Between Cousins
p.175 Jesus Christ

p.176 Jerusalem in the Morning
p.178 The Golan
p.179 Gaza
p.180 The War Casualty
p.181 Israel's Children
p.182 And the Dragon Made War
p.183 Love Most Franked
p.184 Dictators
p.185 The Angel Share
p.186 The Black Madonna
p.187 Sins of Man
p.188 In These Leaves
p.189 October 7th
p.190 Another Forbidden Place
p.191 Candy Canes and Carnivals
p.193 Insomnia
p.194 Beltane
p.195 Grandma's Imagination
p.196 Melancholy Fortune
p.197 The Past Master
p.198 Eyes of Mine
p.199 Way Out Man
p.200 The Robin
p.201 Dank
p.202 Hibernation
p.203 Fresh Morning Air

p.204 I am Listening
p.205 Wonder Hole
p.206 Layer Your Dew Fall
p.207 Fish 'n' Chips
p.208 Coloured Like Rain
p.209 Webs
p.210 The Old Wheel House
p.211 Two Faces
p.212 Homelessness
p.213 Homeless Angel
p.214 Aggi's Gone
p.215 Dartmoor Prison
p.216 A Note to Mr. Magpie
p.217 Solitutued Is
p.218 Musing on Books
p.219 Verity
p.221 Bull Point Light
p.222 The Bogeyman
p.223 The Print Room
p.225 Musing on those Long Summer Days
p.227 Somers Fall
p.228 Somer People
p.230 Red Eyes
p.231 And With It Autumn Comes
p.232 Wind
p.233 Shattered Lives

p.234 Autism
p.235 Great Uncle Ronald and His Combination
p.237 The Flowers
p.238 The Leper's Lane End
p.239 The Trees
p.241 Musing on the Looking Glass
p.242 Wardrobe Talk
p.243 Liberty at Pegasus Bridge
p.244 Fell!
p.245 The Woman of Woe
p.247 Muse on a Loss
p.248 Bude
p.250 Sewers of Life
p.251 Graffiti Poem
p.252 Spirit Moor
p.253 Greystone Memories
p.255 Spirits Having Flown
p.258 Moor at Home
p.259 Tides
p.260 Crossed Over
p.261 A Prison of Love
p.262 Too PC
p.263 Agree
p.264 A Shot of Words
p.265 Lang Dale Muse
p.267 Dad

p.269 Last Kiss
p.270 The Piano
p.271 Along the Granite Way
p.274 Witchcraft
p.275 Viking Queen
p.276 Halo Mary on a Sunday
p.278 A Cloud
p.279 Satan's Approach
p.281 Rafael's Sentiment
p.282 A Take on the Nativity
p.284 When Nephew and Uncle Travel
p.285 The Greatest Story Ever Told
p.287 Lucian Carol
p.288 Rites
p.290 Lydia
p.291 Martha's Poem
p.293 When in Broad Land
p.294 The Dragon at the Door
p.295 Wistman's
p.297 Simply Ted
p.298 Letter to Greta
p.300 Posh
p.302 In the Garden of England
p.303 That Lost Generation
p.304 Blackpool
p.306 Commodore Lady

p.308 Estuary Views
p.310 Diana
p.311 Biglins
p.313 B is 4 Blossom
p.314 The Old Canal
p.315 Mental Health
p.316 The Day After
p.317 The Diagnosis
p.318 Minorities
p.319 For This is All I Know
p.320 Number 9
p.321 On the Eleventh Day
p.322 Easter Day
p.323 The Boat Race
p.324 Public Limited Company
p.325 Encounter
p.327 Ode to Nick
p.328 Nick's Solitary Daughter
p.330 The Recluse
p.332 Patterns of Faith
p.333 The Notion of our Seas
p.334 The Air Raid
p.335 The Worst of Day
p.337 Moorland Japs
p.340 Dandelion Man

THE COMING OF THE WHITE STAG

The Flocking Fox,
And Dancing Ghost Bear,
Ear The Echo,
Of The Bellving White Stag,
For He's Near,
When The Hare Does Dance,
To The Harvest Moon,
For The Old Jay Bird Chatters,
Dropping His Nuts,
For The Squirrel Then,
When In Conversation To The Owl,
The Woodland Is Alive With the Knowing,
For Both The Salmon, Pike, And Otter,
Ear The Coming Of The White Stag,
Is Near,
Blessed Is The Woodland,
For All Those Who Ear,
Let Them Ear,
Meaning Oh Man,
You Are Deaf To Such Things,
                As These,
When As You Are,
Loosing Sleep,
Counting In Your Man-chant House!

BOUDICA

Raise Your Sword,
In Anger.
You Queen Of The Iceni,
Then Make War With The Legions,
                              For Verity,

Arthur,
Merlin,
And Those Celtic's Are As One,
In The West,
With You,

For You Are But The Queen,
Oh Radiant Flat Lander,

Then Enfold The Eastern Winds In Those Skirts,
To Fight And Win,

For The White Stag Is Soon To Appear,
And The Green Man Will Soon Have His Day!!

VIRGINAL HEART

I Saw The Unicorn,
          Then,

Perorating,

In The Golden Meadows,
              There,

Beneath Our Gods Bow,

As White As White,
          Pure,

Like Freshly Driven Snows,
Was It In Innocents,

Virginal,

And Did My Heart Believe,
Coming To The Waters Most Clear,

For It Was Surreal!!

CAROLLING AS ONE WITH THE TRINITY
(A Myth Once Told By Those Early Celtic Saints Of Old)

I am Haunted By The Clouded Girl,
And What Might Have Been?
For It Happened On The Mount,
                Of The Tyrol,

When Peering Into The Lake,
Of Mirrored Love,
Looked Over Then Once Then The Lion Spoke When Roaring,
For He Knew That Which Was Coming,

For The Unicorn And Great White Stag,
Did Dance And Were Seen Together With A Pure Heart,
Whilst As For The Golden Hare,
Well She Just Boxed,

Well As For The Song Of Old John Barley Corn,
Let's Say He Was Just Glad To See His Ole Friend,
In Merriment
That Of The Golden Hare,

In Union With The Unicorn,
And Great White Stag,
Whilst Our Living Waters,
They Giggled And Chucked To The Lovers Call!!

THE UNIVERSAL GARDEN

Surrounded By Climbing Roses,
                        And Walls,

A Child Of The Universe Created A Garden,
And In The Garden Lived A Fairy,
In That Wood That Was Most Contrary,

For It Was A Garden,
Of Tulips In The Spring,
With A Carpet Of Purple Heather Paths,
And A Sherbet Fountain,
Whilst The Perfume Was Thick Of Lavender,
To Dream By On A Pillow Of Sleep,

Then The Fairy Was To Dance With The Dragon Fly,
A Most Lovely Ballet,
Over The River Running Through It,
Which Feed The Garden,
And Lapped With Life,

Whilst At One End Of The Garden,
Were Great Hanging Gates,
And At The End Of The Silver Path,

That Lead From The Gates,
Was The Great White Stag,
Bathed In Light,
For He Was The Light,

And All The Creatures Of The Garden,
       Bow Their Knee To Him!!

THE RAINBOW

The Rainbow Was There,
        Coloured,

In An Over Arching Heaven,
        Shinning,

Is The Promise,
So Our River Flows Quietly Ever On,

Scattering Its Fairy Dust,
        Of Expectation,

Into That New Age,
    After The Rains!

THE ACORN AND THE JAY BIRD

The Acorn and the Jay Bird,
Flapped its Wings,
When once Landing on the Branch,
It Dropped its Sweet Nut,
The Acorn firm and round,
On Landing Swift,
From where Great Oaks,
Our English Oaks would grow,
Side My Journeys Path,
Its colour of Browns and Blue,
Glinted much upon that same Path not known,
When his Eyes were Dark,
And Spied Me so,
Tail Feathers of Darkened White,
Was this a rudder in Flight
Of Autumnal Breeze,

Telling ones of distraction,
There,
Of Winters offing,
For the Jay did not Chirp,
But knew its Season Well,
To comfort,
In the Falling of the Leaves,

That Lie now of Colour,
Being One of Our Forgone Summer,
                              Laid,
Entwine to the Swallows Song!

                    On Seeing a Jay Bird

RAVEN BIRD

Cold Winds Blow,
Cloud over the Sun,
Raven Bird,
Squawks,

19,
Covid-19,

Pestilence Came,
To the Soulless,
      Street!

AT THE HOME OF THE RED SHOE
(Broomhill Near Barnstaple)

And The Red Shoe Danced Alone,
In The Garden,
Just As The Shade,
Like A Hall Of Mirrors,
Stories Told,
With Their Brush,
Sculpted In A Mind Of Languid Lawns
And Watched By The Silver Dragon,
And Golden Hare,
That Said Nothing To The Spirit Of The Wood,
As The River Ran Just As Fast As It Can,
Away From The Two Nude Men,
Playing Their Own Good Tune,
Viewed By The Window,
Whilst Luncheon Was Served.

SMOKE AND MIRRORS

Smoke And Mirrors,
Like A Cigarette,
Puffing,
Is Like Early Morning Mist,
Or As Ones Dreams,
Memories O The Summers
        Since Past,

Now Gone,
Gone,
For We Did Not Know What
        We Had Then,

Until They As The Swallows,
        Had Flown,

Now The Unmentionable Joker,
Come And Sits As
        As The Cuckoo,

Playing With Smoke And Mirrors!

Who Counted The Time And Tide By The Tides Alone,
Spinning Their Silver Threads Out Of Gossamer Wings,

For Even The Queen Of Hearts,
Believed She Would Not Be Queen,
And So She Sat Right Down Next To Our Phoenix,
And Made Him Jam And Cream,
And Spoke with Him In Her Silent Still State,
With The Fairy,
And The Lost Boys!!

MIRACLE ON BOUTPORT STREET

A Woman Falls,
Aggie Cries,
Homeless into Beauty,
Nappies in Town,
Barnstaple Town,
Do Stars Shine,
Old Nick he shouts,
Wining away on his Bottle,
Homeless in Beauty,
Keeping warm,
Keeping Cool,
Does a Mother know,
On selling herself,
When Christmas is comes again,
Homeless into Beauty,
Do the Stars Shine,
In Town,
Barnstaple Town,
Homeless into Beauty.

A QUAKERS VIEW

Why Does A Man Get Meddles Pinned On His Chested?
When All He's Done Is Killed The Foe,
Like The Bloody Hun,
For I'm Sure If They Were To Meet In Peace,
The Two Of Them Would Sit And Share,
And Have A Laugh,
And Generally Commune,
Raising A Glass To Each Others Good Health,
That I Know,

But Oh My Dear,
This Is Wretched War,
This I Know,
For I Don't Really Get,
When Both Have Been At The Alter,
Of Their Lord,
For War Is Just Madness I Tell You,
                                      Madness!

OLD JIM
(Jim Was A Quaker Of Kendal)

If You Should See Old Jim?
Before I Do,
Then Tell The Old Boy,
That I Would Wish To Meet Him,
                              Again!

COCKERMOUTH QUEEN

I Once Knew A Woman,
By The Same Name As My Wife,
                                    Jean,

She Had A Title,
She Was A Lady,
Although it Was As If She Was A Queen To Me,
                       This Cockermouth Lady,

For She Was Interested In Everything I To Am,
Poetry,
Politics,
The Arts,
Religion,
You Could Say Our World In General,

Her Stature Did Not Matter,
Being Blue Eyed Small And Grey,
For She Was Someone That You May Chat To All Day,

There Were Others,
Friendships I Mean,
We Had,

In The Lakes,
Although Known Like Her,
So Forth Right,
In Those Days,
Before Covid Kept Us Apart,
With Just The Telephone Wire To Connect!

Lady Curtis
Jean Curtis
Friend
Died May, '23

THE LIGHTNING SEED

In The Needles Of The Lightning Seed,
Life Is Born,
Golden Purple,
On Derry's Walls,
Necklessing Burning,
Is Hell,
Like A Polo Mint,
        Dark,

For How Can The Lightning Seed,
Respond To This Evil Conductor,
Now Fanning The Flames?
For It's Like Smoke And Mirrors,
One Can No Longer See,
For Surely We All Came Out Of Africa?

OLD COTTONOPLIS

What Old Cottonoplis Does Today,
The UK Does Tomorrow,
With Its Chattering Women,
On Their Weave,

And Row Upon Row Of Back To Back Terraced Houses,
Tumbling In on One Another,
Looking Oh So Weather Beaten In The Drab Conditions,
For The Clouds Are Heavy And Hang Now With Rain,

For Old Cottonoplis Built An Empire Here,
With The Rhythm Of The Cogs,
With Bargy's, Factory Man, And Those Chattering Women,
For The Folks Still Believe Our Streets Are Paved With Gold,

Then Home Or Away Two Tribes Go To War,
Kicking The Hell Out Of An Ole Pig Skin,
Wearing Red And Blue,
Just Like Me And You,

For Who Would Be Up For The Cup,
Come May?
For No One Knows Child,
      At Christmas!!

                              Manchester
                 Second City of the Empire

PUBLIC RANT, SOCIETY NEEDS TO CHANGE, NOT I

Society Needs To Change, Not I,
Do I Have To Travel To Manchester,
Birmingham,
The Isle Of Wight,
Or Even Flaming Glasgow,
Not To Be Crippled,
As You Say,
For You Make Me Disabled,

In What Think,
In How You React,
I see it In Your Face,
You Don't Even Try To Hide It,

The Thing Is,
I am Not Funking Well Handicapped,
But Time And Again,
You Make Me Bloody Well Disabled,
And The Thing Is,
I Call You Friend!

MUSING ON THE STANDING STONES

Standing Stones,
Touch Stones,
Are As Corner Stones,
On Moors,
And Isles Alone,
Weather Blown,
In A Circle,
As In History's Ring,
Telling The Stories,
Of Dancing Myths,
Or Prancing Unicorns,
Or Simple Celtic Folk,
When At Prayer.

LAKE LAND

Windows,
Doors,
And Water Ways,
This Is My Cave,
On The Lakes,
With Fells,
And Mountains,
With All Manner Of Craft,
For The Poets Still Wander,
Look At The Red Squirrel,
See Nutkin Is Alive,
See Both Hardwick,
And Those Who Soar,

Above The Streaming Gill,
Runs The Beck,
Is Great Gable,
Surveying Its Scene,
With Power,
And Weight,
Over Bower Dale,
Not Waving,
But Drowning,
Trapped In Its Rain.

PILGRIMAGE

A Pilgrimage,
Is Like That T. Shirt,
Walked,
And Bought To Day,
Most Spent,
On A Rough And Journey Way,
With Blisters Most Heavy,
Is the Icon Shinning,
Oh Now,
Queen Of Heaven,
Most Chosen,
Look Steps Before Your Road,
Then Be Strengthened Pilgrim,
          Now For Seeing!!

LET GO!

You Are Unhappy,
Then Draw A Mask,
With Me,
Over It,
And Be Entwined With Me,
               Dancing,

Perhaps The Wild Argentine Tango?
For You Alone Cannot Control Third Shocking World,
So Why Do You Try?
Oh My Father,

For Our Sins Have Already Been Dealt With,
Oh My Father,
And St. Michael Has Seen To That,
So My Father,

Let The Music Play On,
And Live Your Life,
In Time With Its Steps,
Very Much To Its Rhythm,
             And Let Go!
                           Dedicated To Dad

HARVEST FESTIVE FARE AT THE NICHOLLS

Tables Were Long,
Tables Were Laiden,
And So We Hurryin' Rabble Sat Down,
Eager To Tuck Right In To Our Festive Fare,
                    Set Before Us,

Although Not Before We'd Spoken Our Amens,
After The Rector Had Said His Word,
Then In The Nicholls Hall Did We Feast,
On Hams, Parsnips, Carrots, Swede And Those
Devon Spuds,
   So Flowery,

All Washed Down Of Course,
With Pitchers Of Scrumpy,
Care Of Old Man Inch,
And The More We Ate,
The More We Drank,
And Loudly Giggled And Laughed Like Drains,
Only To Walk Arm In Arm,
Late That Dark Sky Night,
Shinin' Bright.

For There Should Be No Other Night Like This,

When A Feastin' Rabble As We Were,
Should Sit Down With Rector To Dine Like Kings
That Evenin' Long!!

                          Lydford Harvest Supper
                                    Dartmoor

IN THE DARK TOWN

Gloom,
Hides The Fearful Moon,
To Witchcraft Ways,
Settling Over The Town,
Covering,
Like A Blanket Falls,
Casting Her Spells,
With Dogs A Yelping,
Barking,
Fearing The On Coming Night,

Down Town,
In The Allies And Lanes,
They Duck And And They Dive,
With Drugs And Their Knives,
With The Neon Flicking On,
Pastors And Police Patrol,
Theatre Land,
Club Land,
Oh You're Still Gathering Silent Eye,

With Its Red Lights,
Broken Bottles And Young,
In The Dark Town,

Are You A-Chill?
Cold,
Still,
All Of A Shiver,
For The Dark Town Has Arrived,
Dear One,
      Kind Of Evil My Friend,
              Evil!

IGNORANTS

Surely The Only Thing About Ignorants, Is That It Encourages One To Ask More Questions!

THE FUTURE

The Future,
Our Future,
Is Coming Like An Express Train,
Down The Tracks,
Of Your Tears,
So Get A Board,
Why Don't You?

INSTOW

Playing On The Old Sinking Barge,
                        As We Did,

Into The Sands Of Time,
Running Away With Our Lives,
With The Ferryman Who Had Gone And Crossed Over,

Oh How I'd Still Like To Live At Instow,
As I Did When I Was Just A Boy,
Watching Red Sail,
Ducks And Sunsets,
On Rising And Falling Tides,
With Dreamers And Those With Flowers In Their Hairs,

Oh How I'd Still Like To Live At Instow,
As I Did When I Was Just A Boy,
For Its Twined With Arromanches-le-Bain,
                        You Know,

Oh How I'd Still Like To Live At Instow,
As I Did When I Was Just A Boy,
Hearing Mission Voices Come Rippling In,

On Silver Tides,
Kissing Lapping Our Golden Sands,
Watching Was The Point,
With Those Jealous Eyes!!

                              Instow
                        North Devon
                    Coastal Village

THE JOURNEY

Have You Been On The Rails?
Pulled By The Wonderful Steaming Engine,
For Alongside you are Your Passengers,
Where Are They Going?
What Are They Doing?
And Who Are They?
Travelling On Their Journey,
For Each To Their Own,
      Well I Suppose,

Through Tunnels Of The Mind,
Dark And Forbidding,
Running From The Past,
Into A Brighter Tomorrow,
Crossing Over,
Going One Station Further,
Around Our Next Bend Is The Sunlight,
Of That New Day,
We Wish For,

Speedily On,
Does One Go,
Through The Seasons Of Life,
Not Taking Into Account Your Journey,

A Pleasant One Or Not,
Shall End,
My Friend!

WALKING THE OLD LINE

I'm Sure I Saw A Ghost Or Two,
On The Old Line,
For The Line Had Grown Over,
As For The Rails They Were No Longer There
Now,
Telling Their Stories,
Of Days Gone By,
Tales I Know Which Broke Your Heart,
                        My Dear,

On This Old Branch Line,
For It Is No More Than A Path Of Leisure,
A Trail Through The Woods,
A Glade Of Yesterday,
Through Tunnels Dark,
Unto The Mind,
Out Between Corn Fields Of Views,
Where The Swallows And Swift Dart And Dive,
                        Soaring High,

And So We Joined That Train,
Long Ago,
With Noses Pressed To The Window,
And So The Old Engine,

Like The Author Of The Of Tarka,
Puffed And Puffed,
Black Smoke,
Trying To Catch Up With Yesterday!!

SEA GULLS

Sea Gulls,
Are Really Angels Of The Air,
Leaving Their Feathers,
On The Grasses,
Green,
With Healing Are Their Wings,
Left As Calling Cards,
For It Is They Who Herald The Messages!!

THE JARROW CRUSADE

Oh There's No Hero's Here,
        After Your War,

For There's No Hero's Here,
        After Your War,

There Is No Work Here,
        After The War,

For We're Here And Cold,
Growing Ever Old After That Bloody War,

Building Homes You Promised For Kings,
After That War To End All Wars,

So We're Marching South,
Beneath Our Banners Man,

For We Fought That Wretched Hun,
Beating The Kaiser Men Home Again,

Oh That's Why We're Coming South To London Town,
For Its Where The Rich Boys Live,

NOT COMPLETING

Life,
Is Of Course About Living,
Therefore Of Course We Do Not Complete
    Anything,
Before We Fall Into The Hands Of The Angels!!

WINGS OF DINOSAURS

Child,
Birds Have Wings,
That Of Dinosaurs!!

SOUTHPORT

Red Top,
Head Line News,
See The Fire 'n' Fury,
Southport,
In Anger And Grief,
Grieving,
Do They Mourn,
Laying Flowers,
For Three Little Angels.
Coming Together,
United In Their Pain,
As Tears Fall,
So Ballons Rise,
Rise,
Like That Of An Angel Wing,

For The North Is A Light,
See Again The Fire 'n' Fury!!

Summer, '24

I AM

I am,
MARKED,
By **MAN** Alone!

BARROW ROCK

Well To Whom The B ell Tolls,
Barrow Rock Will Be,
A Far To Shore,
A Marker,
For Who They Are,
In Telling Tides,
Of Oceans Swell,
Batterin' The Rock So Grey,

For The Folks Go A-Wanderin' Summerleaze
Sands Of Mists,
Where Once The Bede did Land Sit To Preach,
Here Within This Celtic Kernow Kingdom
Strong,
Showin' Mercy Of The Lord,
        Is Just Swell!!

                        Bude

VOYAGE

All I Pray,
Oh Traveller,
Be Strong Sound Enough,
For The Crossing,
Whilst You Shall Come Against Hazards
                              And Risks,

Of Storms And Rocks,
To Sawy The Ship,
Hold Firm The Helm,
And Push On,
For I Give Thanks,
That The Land In Which You Seek,
                 Is None To You!

KITES

Have You Seen The Kites?
Smiling,
So High In The Sky,
Wafting,
With Their Tales,
Are Their Faces,
Is Their Life,
A Life Of Their Own,
Like A Fairy Tales,
On Gusts 'n' Breezes,
Always Moving On,
Over Our Parks,
And Shoreline Sands,
Of My Dreams,
Where The Lion And The Unicorn Live,
        At Peace And Liberty!!

DOROTHY'S GARDEN

Painted Lady,
Bird or Angel,
I know not,
Which,

A single Feather lies,
in front of the Sun,
Near,
Tranquil water,
A Garden to be hold,
Summer's perfume of fragrant
                          Sweet,

Of climbing Rose,
Trees do Bloom,
Giving Shade,
The Waning Shadows Lengthen,
              Days are Cast,

Where Wild Life feeds,
Sometime from the Hand,
In your Garden of pure delights,
                "Dorothy"
There is Time,

Time,
To Pause,
Take a Chair,
For Sherry 'n' a Snooze,
On Emerald Camomile Lawns,
In your Garden,
Your Beloved Garden,
Of Cornish Air.

For Dorothy

WOMEN

Women,

The Great Daughter,

The Nice Niece,

The Pleasing Partner,

The Wonderful Wife,

The Digital Mother,

Then The Happy Granny,

Comes The Infirm,

Women,

Doing No More!

LOOKING GLASS

Women,
      Function As A Looking Glass!

CATARACT

Waterfall!

SOCIAL MEDIA

And Now We Shout At Each Other,
Loudly,
With Anger In Our Hearts,
Causing Pain,
And Hurt,
Through The Ethe,
Unseen,
Called Out From The Shadows,
Of That Dark Web,
Haunting Other Folks,
Is That Graffiti like Sickness,
With Green And Yellow Pruck,
                On The Mind!

THE DRAGON AWAKENS
(Based, You Reader, On Revelation)

Splits The Stone,
Oh Sinful Man,
When Statues Fall,
Slapping Idols,
Tasting Fruit,
Your Gods Are Coming,
          Welcome,

Brings Dirty Insight,
Coloured,
Of Stained 'n Sacred Souls,

Washed Are The Martyrs,
Whilst Rejoicing,
Their Scared Raiments,
     Shining Brightly,

Entrenched,
You Earth,
In Your Pains,
Oh Painted Harlot,
Of Hells Great Knowing,
Recites The Repeating Number

When Smokes The Face,
Is The Dragon's Hate; Now Appearing,
With Him Once Again; His Chimera,
When Making Nations Conflict; Groaning,
You Warrior Of Mars,
Brings You Michael,

To Cast Him Out!

THE KREMLIN'S CABAL
(Invasion Of Ukraine '22)

Red Mist Rising,
The Bear Is Stirring,
Wakening From His Slumber,
                    Beware,

The Animal Comes,
Roaring,
Warring,
Consuming a Neighbour,
        Mired In Blood,

The Bear Is Stirring,
And Now We See Him For What He Really Is,
That Of The Kremlin's Cabal,

                Dear Children,
                Dear Children!

FOUR HORSEMEN
(The End Of Time)

When Four Horsemen Were Approaching,
The Earth Was Scorching,
Burning,
Temperatures Were A-Rising,
Higher By The Season,
With The Seas A-Rising,
For The World Was Spinning,
      Out Of Control,
          Control,

As Those Prophets Were Telling,
Poler Ice Was Thinning,
As The Darkness Covered The Sun,
So Lucifer Fell,
To His Fiery Kingdom,
With His Harlot,
Scarlet,
Proud,

And Dancing,
Bringing With Her,
War And Famine,
When Four Horsemen Were Approaching!

MICHAEL

Oh Michael's Gone To Slay The Dragon,
Red With Blood,
And Purple Veins That Dragon Was Kicked Into Touch.
And Stained With Sin,
He Fell For Ten Thousand Years,
To Earth He Fell,
Into That Land Of Fire,
Where Michael Would Slay Him Upon The Hill,
Knowing The Healing Of The Nations Would Then Begin!!

BIRTHDAY WISHES

It's Never Oh So Big Or Clever,
To Drink A Load Of Beer,
Or To Wobble Around Like Some Bloody Cripple,
Then Grin With That Gin,
From Ear To Ear,
For If you do one Shall Talk A Load Of Nonsense,

Nor Is It To Clever,
To Fall Down On Your Fat Ass,
But One Must Confess,
It Is Bloody Good Fun!!

GET INKED

JuSt,
GeT,
    'INKED'
wHy,
    Don'T,
yOu?

WiTh BuTtErFlIes,

Is YoUr,

    'Tattoo'

Is Your Graffiti
    Drawn,

You Who Are,
Of This TaTtOoEd Nation Sweet,

    'AlBiOn Street'

Your Men Will March,
And Answer Your Call,
    To Battle WhEn!

TEDDY
(A Child Reminiscences)

Teddy On the Bed,
Speaks to Me,
Of Happy Day,
Oh Happy Day,

Sun Glints Through My Pane,
        Open Pane,

On to The Cipher Frame,
With Cars and Toys Arranged,
Thunderbirds Are Go,
Lady Penelope,
All Along, Penny Lane,
        My Lane,

Watching Moon Landings,
        And Nam,

Through My Pain,
Open Pain,
Is Hippy, Hippy Time,
Teddy on the Bed!

        Dedicated To David Bell

FIRST FOOTING

Hot Coals,
First Footing,
Are We,
Making Merry,
Is The Sound Of The New Year Bell,
Causing Chaos,
Through The Vale,
Hardly Recovering From The Yule Tide Blessing,
As We Make One Joyful Noise,

See Grandpa There On The Stair,
He's Grabbed Mothers Tray,
And He's Sliding Down The Stair,
For Kissing Mary Jane!!

*I Took Part In This At
Lydford, Devon, Late-80's*

THE ORPHAN

Oh How You Long To Be The Child,
At Play,
In School,
But Your Not,
Your Facing The World,
Smiling,
Alone In The World,
For You Are The Orphan,
Left As A Reflection,
In A Hall Of Mirrors,
For The Morning,
      Will Come!

WHEN THE MOON AND THE TIDE COME UP TO SAY GOODBYE

Please Bring Me Back,
Bring Me Back,
      Here,

After The Children,
And The Families,

After The Summer,
And The Wild Parties,

For The Sun Will Still Be Hot Then,
When The Students Being To Creep Back Then
With The Driftwood

And Tide,

Please Bring Me Back,
Bring Me Back,
      Here,

Where The Airs Are Calm Upon The Wing,
And Paradise Shall Be Found Around The Next
Corner,

On Lapping Sands As Silver,
With Windows And Dreaming Spires Of Fortune,

Please Bring Me Back,
Bring Me Back,
      Here,

To The Lizard Peninsula,
Where The Mermaids Sing,

At Old Porthleven,
And Miss. Daisy Is Still Serving Well At The Duchy,

So Pray Ye,

Please Bring Me Back,
Bring Me Back,
      Here,

Lord,
With A Pole Star To Shine!!

Written At
The Royal Duchy Hotel Falmouth
Sept, '24

FISH TIDES AND THE SEA WEED

Fish Tides And The Sea Weed,
Brought By Neptune,
Upon Old Albion's Ancient Shoreline,
Is Flotsam And Jetsam,
The History Of Yours And Mine,
Once Told,
Now Stranded Beached Like Maids,
Lost In Tides Of Man's Desiring!

GLOSSOP WARD

Illness,
Sickness,
And disease,
A Man is in his bed,
Laying,
Laying,
To death us do part,
He struggles to breathe,
   Struggles to breathe,

Quietly,
He coughs on his cylinder,
He coughs on his cylinder,
Just as Robin,
The Gay Nurse approaches,
And comes in the Night,
And comes in the Night,
Taking his Temperature,
Like an Angel,
For washing his Bottom,
   Washing his Bottom,

Patience,
Life is like a Hell whole,

And you still need your Mum,
When Life is like a Piece of Shit,
Just when you're in Jobs Pit,

Then along comes a Man,
With Beads, Crosses 'n' Prayers,
Crosses 'n' Prayers,
And that Collar he wears,
He wears,
Saying, A men,
A men,
A men.

My Illness 2012

IN THE WAITING ROOM
(Very Poorly 2012)

Once I Was Ill.
Once I Was Dying,
In A Ward,
That Had A Station,
With No Rails,
Was That Very Room,
Where Illness And Death,
Did Stalk In Silence And Pain,

Oh This Was My Window,
On A World Of Shattered Dreams,
In A Waiting Room Such As This,
Of Oxygen One Gasped And Gasped Their Last,

As Did I,
In A World Of Ever Decreasing Walls,
Grabbing At Pills,
And Potions,
Whilst Being Spoon Feed Our Lord,
However, I Might Have Convinced Him At The Time?
For Although Visitors Came And Went,
Time Was Not My Own,

As I Wrestled With The Dark Angel,
And All His Wonderful Tricks!

I'M A POET

I'm A Poet,
A Sage,
So There,
And Don't I Know It,
Slightly Rebellious,
Left Wing,
So There,
But Awfully Loveable,
You Know,

So I'm Bloody Well Going To Swear,
On The Great River Styx,
Mr. Ferryman,
For Even The Gods Can't Do That,

              So Fuck Off!!

TURNED

And She Turned Her Face Away!

Mother And
Her Dementia

TV

TV,

Is the Box In The Corner,
That Just Teaches You To Idol Your Time Away,
At A Very Early Age,
Get One Thing Straight,
Its Bloody Boring,
Listen To The Wireless,
Or Better Still Open A Book,
Of Chapter And Verse,
Learn,
Discover A New World,
Of Spell Binding Future,

As For TV,

You Don't Want Any More Flaming Repeats,
        Do You?

HAVE YOU SEEN THE MAGICAL COLOURS IN THE RAIN

Have You Seen The Magical Colours In The Rain?

PUCK

Young Puck Has Been Around For ever,
He's Nothing But A Contradiction In Terms,
Looking So Cherub Like,
Although Young Puck Is A Very Nowty Fairy,
Hypnotic With His Eyes A -Bright,
                And Wonder, I'll

Casting Spells,
Over Them That Come,
To The Woodland – Deep Dark And Magical,

Puck He's Such A Will Of The Wisp,
He's A Demonic Little Fairy-Chap,
Jumping Out Through History,
Causing Colourful Chaos 'n' Rhyme,
Oh Puck Will Make You Dance All Night,
                All Right,

The Horrible Little Fellow,
With That His Sweet Smile,
He's No Cherub,
Its Magic,
You Know,

  Magic,

Fear It My Love,
Fear It,
For It Will Lead You A-Stray!!!

>Dedicated To
>The Bard Of Stratford

JULIAN

Damn burst of Dreams,
Angels don't have Wings,
My darling,
Clothed in Green,
Like a Postman,
Oh how obscene,
        He Said!

                                            May 17th, 1995
                                           When An Angel
                                                Appeared
                                                    To Me!

WHITE FEATHER

Is My White Feather Lying There?
Oh Angel OF Mine,
You're Still There,
On The Turf,
Staying True,
My Julian,
You're No Phantom,
I Have Touched you,
At St. Stephen's,
Have You Been Here All Night?
Whilst I Sleep,
For I Thank you,
My Julian!

DARK WATER

Our Water,
Is Deep,
Dark,
Quiet,
Black,
Still To Day,
Seemingly Not Moving,
Has The World Stopped Today?
                      Of All Days,

It's Kind Of Mysterious,
As If The Earth Waits,
Uncanny Like!!

THE SEA

A Lone Gull Cries,
For It Can't Be Tamed,
      You Know,

Its Wild,
Evil,
Taking Souls,
Upon The Rock,

For It Can't Be Tamed,
      You Know,

With Mists Swallowing Mists,
Amid The Churning Surf,
Casting,
Throwing Stones,

When Arises The Great Leviathan,
Showing Its Ugly Head,
Then Neptune Shall Ride Upon It Back,

Haunting,
Haunting,
Crying Like The Lone Gull!

TO THE QUEEN OF CRIME FICTION

You Worked In A Hospital,
And Once I Lived In The Same Town As You,
                              Woman,

Whose Brother Lived In A Castle,
Pulled By An Amazing Goat,
              My Dear,

For In Your World,
Things Are Never What They Appear To Be?
For The Gunman Is Behind The Door,

Archie,
Then She Married You,
Just Before You Went To That,
              Glorious War!

MY CREED

Oh I Believe In The Man In The Clouds,

With Saints And Angel Wings,

In The Sky,

Casting Showers And Bows,

For Once He Walked With Men,

Even Walking On The Sea,

Just So You Know,

Surround By Pleasant Meadows,

A Wash With Breakfast,

Of Crystal Streams,

Where Unicorns Play And Dance,

With Golden Harp And Liar,

And Fairy Stories Told In Rhyme,

Once Told,

Amid A Chorus Of Voice,

Like So!!

THE STATUE

Beauty And Form,
Shone Through,
Curved,
With Angle,
And Poise,

For Then Our Statue Fell,
To The Floor,
Swished By The Cat,
Naked Did She Fall,

And Broke,
Shattering The Silence!

Whilst Grown And Playing In The Park!

Ashley & Nathan

THE CATHEDRAL

The Cathedral Had Three Spires,

The Cathedral Has Its Alter,

The Cathedral Had A Screen,

The Cathedral Has Its Lady Chapel,

The Cathedral Had An Organ,

The Cathedral Had A Choir,

The Cathedral Had Its Windows-Stained At That,

The Cathedral Had The Bishop And The Dean,

The Cathedral Has Its Great West Door,

The Cathedral Had Its Guides,

Its Then We Ask,

Where Is Jesus Love?
For A Lonely Woman Sings Yonder Door!!

FLAVOUR

It's Cheese And Onion,
Wacky St. Peter!!

I GIVE

I Give,
Of Myself,
History,

For The Young,
Think,
History,
Started With Them!!

FLATLAND-FENLAND

Magic Eels,

You Broad Open Skies,
Blow Gently The Corn,
Golden Faced,
Ripening,

Murmurs You Waters,
With The Sounds Of Mise And Men,
To Which Your Airs Do Reply,

Upon Their Wing,
See You Ship,
Oh You Great Ship,
Of The Fens,

You Ancient People's Of The Fens,
                Iceni's Children!!

BE A BROADCASTER

BE A BROADCASTER!
E
A
B
R
O
A
D
C
A
S
T
E
R!

DOES ANYONE HAVE A GREEN HEART?

In The Falling O The Leaves,
Rotating Into The Coming Season,
                    Once Again,

Time Had Passed Once More,
Now Grief Clouds The Night,
Most Born Of Your Day,
Asked Of You,

      Does Anyone Have A gREEN

HEART?

                                    Enquire Of Grenfell
                                        Seven Years On

PHONE CALL FROM MY FRIEND

He Began To Speak,

Sharply,

Harshly,

It Wasn't Him,

Neither Were The Words,

Being Rapid-Quickly-Spaced,

Intent On Getting His Message Over,

His Words Now More Of A Chatter,

Drawing For Breath-He Sighed,

His Words Became A Chitter,

Pouring The PRUCK From Him,

He Was A Very Worried, Worried Man,

And Now He's Not The Only One!!

Wishing Grenville Well

WINDOWS ON THE WORLD

Windows On The World,
Wheels For The World,
Is Your Paralympics,
Now Oh London 2012,
Oh Show Case,
Then Go Blade Runner Go,
Running In This Show Case,
A Festival Of Flame!!

ROUGH WATER

Oh My Father,
I'm Sailing The Water,
Rough Water,
Whilst Carrying Your Cross,
Away From The Skull,
To Get To Jordan's Side!

IN THIS THE BEAUTIFUL HOUSE OF BAILEY

Up From Its Lapping Cove,
Is A House I Know W ell-A Pilgrims Rest,

Here There Is A Joy Of Being,
                   At Peace,

A Holy Peace,
In And Around This Building,

As Mist Lingers,
Like Vapour-Wafting,

Spirits Of Blessing,
For The Day,

Hark Early I Hear Music,
And Prayer-Gentle Like,

Ascending,
Nestling-In This The Beautiful House Of Bailey!!

                                    Lee Abbey
                                        Devon

LEE ABBEY

The air is clear Hear,
Kind of Whispering still,
Is its Silence,
High,
With Octag,
And Chapel Cove,
Beautiful is the House of
                Bailey,

For here is a Thin place,
When entering into His doors,
Spirit and Waters Quench,
                Lapping,

Breaking Bread together,
Nations Commune,
Whilst Angels Listen,
From a distant Realm,
            Appearing!

Lee Abbey Fellowship
Devon

OH BLESSED ARE THE POOR

Oh How The People Are Poor,
Poor In Hunger,
And Poor Of Spirit,
        Lord,

What With The Mortgage,
'Tis a Nothing But A Mill Stone,
Around Ones Neck,
All That They Mean You To Do,
Is Work, Work, Work,

Oh Blessed Are The Poor,

Now You Queuing For Your Bread,
And All,
At Some Church Run Food Bank,
And You're Not At All Religious,
Just Hungry,
You Hunger For Fairness,

Oh Blessed Are The Poor,

Amid The Various Kinds Of Abuse,
Oh Blessed Are The Poor!!

SOMETHING IS WRONG MINISTER

The People Are Behind With Their Mortgage,

The People Cannot Pay Their Bills,

For The People Are Turning Off Their Heating,

For The People Are Using Food Banks,

And Some Of These Do Work,

For Something Is Wrong Minister,

When Kids Come To School Without A Breakfast,

For Now There's Trouble In The Middle East,

Minister,

And What Do You Propose To Do About These Things?

SILVER RIVER RAIN

Glistening,

Silver River Rain,
Twinkling
Rippling,
In The High Spring Tides,

Genteel Is The River,
Slow,
Under Our Rainbow,
There Were Faces Here,
And Faces There,
People Were Insecure,

As There Silver River Rain,
Just Flowed,
Constant,
And Said Nothing,
To The Ashen White Faces,
Who Just Looked-bemused,
At Their River,
Trapped As They Mellow In The Quite Hills,
And So I Guess It Would Weave Its Timeless Story!

GOLDEN BROWN

The Air Is Still Now,
The Excitement Of The Fair Is Over,
      Done For Another Year,

As Those In The Fields,
Have Gathered In The Sheaves,
Rejoicing At The Spreads Before Them,

As The Sun Turns Its Face Away,
Trees Are As Golden Brown,
For The Hedge Row Harvest Is Laden,

When The New In Take Begins,
So I To Do Think Of My Great Niece,
Just As Heavenly Bodies Are Seen Over Greece,

For Things Are On The Change As They've
Always Been,
Just As We Remember Them,
And So The Winter Storms Will Come,

Light The Fire Then,
And So Keep The Witches Away,
Drawin' Near To 'Ear The Stories Of Old My Dear.

THE LAST DREGS OF SUMMER

Oh I Was Happy Then,
When All Things Seemed Mellow,
And Slow,
For It Was Autumn Then,
And I Smiled,
Catching The Last Dregs Of Summer,
For The Sun Shone Brightly,
Through The Wavering Trees,
                            Then,

Whilst I Did Drink The Amber Apple,
Tasting Summers Golden Fruit!

POETRY IN THE RAIN

Poetry In The Rain,
Spoke To Me Softly In The Rain,

Watching The Animals As We Did,
In The Rain,

Whilst We Danced Our Way Between Rough Sleepers,
In The Rain,

Listening To The Laughing Drains,
In The Rain,

Know That Our Chains Of The Seas Had Been Busted In The Night,
In The Rain,

For The White Stag Played His Nation Guitar,
In The Rain,

And Guarding The Stumps Of The Chains Of The Tree,
Were The Marching Men Of The Busbed Hats,
In The Rain.

THE WATER OF LIFE

The Water Of Life,
Sprang Forth,
Hidden Deep In The Garden,
And It Was Called Whiskey,
Which Can Be A Firm Friend,

A Pet,
Ageing Slow,
Kind Of Mellow,
Were Those Malts,
Maturing,
Evolving,
Is The Angel Share,

To Taste,
When Opened,
From The Oak Casts,
Then Drink,
With Your Fine Cigar!

SOLSTICE POEM

Darkness,
Fearful,
And cold,
Bewitching is the Light,
Broken of Twigs,
Comes Crow foot,
In the Snow,
Is the Colour White,
For Our Light always comes back,
                    Comes back,

Spills you over,
Turning Point,
Wintering Solstice,
Until then We will Kiss the Moon,
Dance then Shadowing Light,
Carolling through,
You Lord of Miss Rule,
When frosted is Our Pain,

White is the Stag,
That is seen,
              Retuning!!

WINTER HAS SETTLED NOW

Winter Has Settled In Now,
As If A Blanket,
Is Over The Park,
The Trees Are As If They To Are Charcoal
Statues,
Speaking To Each Other
As They Know Best,
Conjuring Up A Greek-Co Roman World Of
Myths,
In The Silence,
For Had Someone Put A Spell On It,
Frozen For The Storms Begin,
Do You Think?
For The Winged Ones Pad The Ground,
In The Hope Of A Morsel,
Whilst We Expect The Lord Of Miss Rule,
In The On Coming Snows,
Being As Old Age As It Is,
Just As The Squirrels Go To Their Nuts.

THE YELLOW STAR

Our World Is Made By Little Miracles,
By The People Of The Yellow Star,
However Did The Germany Not See Recognize That?
Or Did They?
And Did They Envy Them Much?
Those People Of The Yellow Star,
For They Are The Chosen Ones,
Picked Out From The Oh From The Nations!!

THE DREAMLESS SLEEP

No Longer Do You Play,
With Fairy Dust,
A Long The Blackberry Lane,
For Winter Came,
Suddenly,
Bringing With It,
The Stare Of The Dreamless Sleep!

THE LOST GENERATION

All Gone To God,

Women Lost Husbands
Brothers And Lovers,

They Were Scythed Down,
In There Season,

For The Lost Generation,
Did Not Return Home,

Now Their Names Lie,
Row Upon Row,

Like Little Soldiers,
All On Parade!

The Great War
1914-18

SHADOW ON MY MIND

Shadow On My Mind,
Like A Cloud On My Mind,
Is Angels And Spirits Walking,
Haunting On My Mind,

Shadow On My Mind,
Like A Cloud On My Mind,
By Of Tatters Of Parents,
      All Hung Over,

For I Taste Your Vodka,
And Of Your Rum,
Waiting For A Shipment Of Tobacco And Gin,
In This The Witches Town,
Where Angels And Spirits War,
On Blackened Chuckling Cobbles,
Come The Night Of The Blue, Blue Moon,
During That Night When Stepping Through All Hallows,
Eve My Love,

So Just Take Care!

OH PLEASE REMEMBER

Oh Please Remember This Now,
You Can Not Look At The Sun For Long,
Nor At Death Very Long,
For Its Mask Hides A Thousand Secrets,
                                          Darling!

MOVING ON

And Summer Past!

SODOM AND GOMORRAH COMES TO TOWN

Oh Days Of Wine And Drunkenness,
Come To Our Small Town,
        Final Days,

Of Which There Are Many,
Among The Black And Miserable Faces,
Oh Sodom And Gomorrah,

Men Do Drugs,
Woman Selling Themselves,

Men In Bed With Men,
Women With Women,

Others In Doorways,
To A Locked World To The Future,

The Abused Remain Silent,
Here Amid Their Screams,
In The Night Of Their Days,

For The Child Are Running Scared.
Little Bethlehem Of Galilee,
As For The Boogeyman He's Alive And Well!

MARY'S POEM

How Many Men Have You Had?
                Oh Mary,

And Do They Pay You Well
For Your Services?

Or Do They Abuse You?
           Oh Mary,

For You Have Never Loved A Rabbi Before
                          Have You?

And One Who Turns Water Into Wine,
                Oh Mary,

For There Are None Like Him,
            To Compare?

Oh Mary!!

                                  Mary Magdalen

DESTINY'S DREAM

A Chorus Of Angels Of Men,
Spoke Of Tales Of Glory,
Whilst Fairy's Live Forever,
But Not So Rites Of Man,
Even If They Are Called Arthur,

Now That Destiny Has Fled From The Garden,
Through Lavender Fields Of Blue,
She Wandered Dwelling On What Might Have Been,
And Her Skies Were As Her Golden Bangles,

For Destiny And Her Unicorn,
Did Go Afar To The Lost Land Of Lioness,
                                        My Dear,

For Our Queen Of Hearts Had Lost Her Crown,
When Tossing Her Toys From The Pram,

Whilst Out Of The Thin Air,
Swooped Old Mrs. Magpie,
And Stole Those Wretched Jewels Away,
To Line Her Own Nest,
                Did She,

For Then Our Fortunes Were Told,
Long Time Since Ago,

Just When The Unicorn,
Bound The Wounds,
Of The Struggling Nations,
And So Dear Destiny Sang Her Song,
Whilst That Unicorn Played His Harp
                            Along,

Then Mere Martha The Mermaid Did Appeared,
From Her Cave,
Along With Old Giant Bumble Weed,
Now In Toe,

And Then The Green Man Withered Away,
Away Forever And A Day,

Knowing A New Age Was Coming,
For It Was A Good Morning In Spain!!

SHE WHO WEEPS FOR ME

The Black Madonna,
Is The One Who Weeps For Me,
In All Her Sexual-ness,
Torn In Two Behind Those Bars Of Iron,
There Is But Human Flesh,
Distant In The Rains,
Bejewelled Like Some African Queen,
Spilling Her Many Tears,
On The Healing Of The Nations,
Wish She Could Do On More,
For Those Many Coloured Faces!!

LONG TIME COMING

Swallows,
They're A Long Time Coming,
      Casting Shadows,

Summer Time Long Time Coming,
Of Golden Rays,
Neither Shall Stay,

Of Brittle Gardens,
And Unicorns!!

ABORTION

SMELL,

Spell,

Go On,

That Wretch Ugly Word,

!!ABORTION!!

ALCOHOL

Oh Woe is Me My Friend,
Of years such past,
I started to Drink,
Around My Teens,
Upper Teens,
On that Stool,
Set aside for Me,

Half a Cider,
A Pint of Shandy,
Bitter,
Was their Taste,
Then Port and Lemon,
Came the Sherry,
For it made Me Merry,
For I was a Social Drinker,
Drinking with the Chaps,
The Chaps of the Village,

Down at the Inn,
The old Castle Inn,
Smelling Tobacco,
Most Fine,
My Friends,

Buying Me,
And Plying Me,
Buying Me,
And Plying Me,

Leading Me a stray,
        A Stray,

For the Chase, the Hunt was not yet Begun,
                                        Begun.

SMOKING IN BED

Lying,
Pondering,
Nearly In The Dream Time,
Being Intoxicated,
Just Smoking In Bed,
The Blue Smoke Rise,
Making Yellow Stains On The
                        Ceiling,

Oh My Dearest St. Edmund,
Brave Knight Of The Table!

HAVE YOU READ ME?

Have You Read The Writing On My Face?
Have You Been Where I Have Been?
Do You Know It Well?
Only To Taste Bitter Herbs,
For I Feel Tired And Weary,

Have You Read The Writing On My Face?
For It Is Like This,
I am Somewhere I Rather Not Be,
Talking In Bed,
Being The Nightmares Of Dreams,

Have You Read The Writing On My Face?
Bearing The Pain Of My Christ,
Living Here Out In The Community,
Witnessing For Him,
With All My Faults,
And All,

For Yes I'm Here,
Disabled,
Crippled,
And Still Standing,
For There Is One In Four Of Me,

So Don't Go Putting A Label On Me,
Anyway I'm In Your Bloody Face!!!

IT'S ANOTHER DAY

Night,
When All Is Still,
Its Another Day!

WITH ME!

Pain,
Is with ME!

HARTLAND QUAY

Hartland Quay Then In Autumn Light,
'Twas Kind Of Erie Then,
In Fading Light,
When I Did Once Climb Down To That Cove,
From The Well Known Inn,
Cast With Smugglers Tales Then,

Its Light To Sea-Fares Warned,
Ships Away From Ugly Jagged Rocks,
For Our Cliffs Were Tall 'n' Like A Layer Cake,

For I Call It Ours For I Am A Man Of This Clay Of Devon,
Oh Such Aged Prehistoric Crumblin' Soil Of Cliffs So High,
Oh Again Raised In Torrent Times We Did Not Know,
For Once The Poets Long Ago Did Tell,
Like I,

And Old Harland's Plough Boy To Priest,
Did Miracles Throughout His Journeys Way!!

GHOST BEARS

Blonde on Blonde,
Is Our Sun,
Fading,
As the Skies then turns Pink,
Pink with Delight,
So Pink,
When Our Birds went home to Roost,
The Squirrels scampered from Tree,
              To passing Tree,

Whilst at the Bottom,
Rooted and Snorted,
The Ghost Bears,
The Ghost Bears,
Haunting,
for ridging,
At Play,
At Play,

In Our Twilight Zone,
As first Dusk,
Then the Night,
Settled,
To Merge with the Night,

The Dark Sky Night,

For the Ghost Bears would come,
Would Come,
Deep from their Sets,
Deep from their Sets,

Ghost Bearing,
Ghost Bearing,
Is this Woodland Picture,
A Marvel,
Merging with Cattle and the Night,
Cattle and the Night,
Spreading decease,
Or Not?
Decease or Not?
Rooting Snorting questioning a Life,
                              a Life,

Of the Ghost Bears,
Ghost Bears,
Haunting,
Telling their Tales of the Forest Floor,
Forest Floor,
When the Vixen Screamed,
Screamed Aloud,

And the Love Owl Flew,
Flew,
A silent White,
To Hunt,
To Hunt,
And To Watch!

Walking Through The Woods At Twilight Time
Lydford

IT'S THAT CHEEKY BEAR POEM

The Bear Watched The Butterfly,
                    There,

Perching Upon His Nose,

But What The Bear Did Not See,

Is The Hornet,

On His Rear,

For The Hornet Bit Him Then Upon His
BUM!!

'AND THAT'S

A VERY cheeky Bum poEM!'

SHE'S A WALDORF SUPER STAR

She's A Waldorf Super Star,
She Is,
She Is,
That Had Exploded Like Apollo,
On To The Silver Screen,
When There Was To Many Actors,
                         Stage Right,

And Not Enough Directors,
In This The Age Of Aquarius,
When The Gods Of Old,
Walked With Mortals,
Down Our Cobbled Lanes,
Fast Was That Dance,
When Carolling Then Together,
For The Stars Were In Line,

When Our Waldorf Super Star,
Sang Out,
Dazzling Her Heals,
And Strutting Her Stuff,
In Time With The Stars,
When Falling From Favour,

For It Was Then,
Venus Turned Her Face Away,
When At once Upon That Day,
She To Had Twinkled Lightly,
For To Clasping With Jupiter And Mars!!

THE GLASTONBURY CALL

Glastonbury,
Kingdom Of Avalon,
Colour,
Your Abbey,
Spoken In The Spirit,
In Perfumed Mysticism To Merlin,

Where Once An Uncle Brought His Nephew,
From A-Far,
Tells His Story Does The Tree,
When Dances The Solstice,
Comes The Festival,
Beneath The Pyramid Stage!

OBSERVATION POEM

I Have Observed Man,
And All His Many Moods,
Beneath Those Hats,
That He Wears,
Looking So Distinguished,
                And All,

Then Again I Have Observed Man,
Wearing His Coloured Masks,
Under Those Laughing Faces,
              Which He Chooses,

"Amaris".

THE OLE SILVER FOX AND HIS STORY

In Our Small Hours,
When All Were A Sleep,
The Ole Silver Fox,
Did Cross The Road,
Where There Are No Fences Facing,
In Shadow Mist To Desire,

That Rummage From The Trash,
Outside beneath The Gates Of The Old Rectory,
Whilst Father Mathews Lay Deep A Sleep,
Dreaming Of That Woman Who He Left,
On Derry's Walls,
Now In Ruin,
For Lack Of Love,
Dear Ruben Mathews,

And So The Ole Silver Fox,
Did Chew Upon Father Matthews Old Sermons
And Notes,
Leading The Owl In Her Tree,
To Think That The Ole Silver Fox Maybe
Cunning,
Or Was He Trying To Seek Biblical Redemption?
For Those Sins He Has Done In His Time,

The Ole Silver Fox,

Just As Nicodemus Came One Night,
To Jesus,
And Then Did The Astronaut Go Sailing By,
As If On Galilee
Raising His Great And Good Hands,
With A Men?

THE GRIFFINS TALE

Have You Heard The Legend?
For Once Upon A Time,
A Splendid Griffin Came This Way,

And Did This Griffin With Golden Wings,
Fly High In The Awesome Sky,
Not Once,
But Thrice,
With Pegasus,
For Settling Near That Golden Fleece,

A-Then Joining Sir Robert Of Locksley,
And His Merry Men,
Hiding In The Tree,
Except For Young Will,
The Scarlet Capped One,

For The Griffin So Golden,
Escaped Noah's Great Flood,
And When The Coloured Bow Appeared,
For All To See,
This The Golden Griffin,
Did Make Himself Scarce,
Although This The Griffin Shall Reappear,

Toward The End,

Most Wired,
Don't You Think?

THE SILENT ISLAND ACORN TREE

Wet was the day
Rainy day, and Monday.
When I did kick an' scuff at the leaves
That had fallen from the trees,
Neath the cool breezes blow.
When days roll into Weeks an' Weeks
Into Months and begotten Years.

For I am sick, sick to death,
Tired an' weary,
Weary an' worn
Tattered an' torn,
To shreds of life
Here after death,
All duty bound.
Where floating flutterin' fools
Exist only for the silly most rules.

What is the purpose?
What is the time?
In this realness of rhyme.
When moody is the home
Of the silent Island acorn tree,
That has cast its shadow a far to Sea.

Both opening an' closing
Rising an' falling,
To the tide about
This shrouded shaded silent Island of an acorn tree.
That has stood through time
Above all benign an' mindless rhyme,
In all its perfect honesty.

Where Cathedrals an' temples
They stand an' they lie,
In ashes of ruin.
Our silent Island acorn tree
Will still be standing eternally.

THE PILGRIM, SAINT, AND THE UNICORNS HORN

Oh A Pilgrim Came A-Dancing Then,
One Day,
Around The River Eden Most Fair,
To Lay His Alms Before The Saint,
Buried There,
His Alms Were That Most Precious Unicorns
Horn,
He Lay Before The Saint,
Instead Of Silver Or Gold,
For He Did Desire Much,
That Pilgrim,
Who Came A-Dancing Then,
For That Said Pilgrim,
I Confess My Friend,
Was I,
Most Lame,
With Spastic Claw,
Did Asked Hugely For A Miracle Then,
To Be Performed,

From Beyond The Grave,
Oh Saintly One!!

Whilst In Durham

THE PEREGRINE

Mirror and the Light,
Fell like a Shadow,
For the Peregrine,
Fell,
Swooping,
And Soaring,
Did the Gyre,

Floating on Sky Songs Air,
For this was his Element,
Dropping and Diving,
When Hunting at Speed,
        For to Kill,

The Wood Cock was already Dead,
Blood Stained was its Death,
A Noble Death,
Gave up its Field,
For that was the way of its Earth,
        Circling,

Circling,
Did the Peregrine Feed,
Tearing,

With Beak and Talons,
On his young Cock,
For the Morrow had not yet come,
It to would Die of its Fortune,

And the gods in their Gilded Cages,
Looked this Way,
Though did nothing,
But watched,
As the Hedgerow was Sherrill,
With Wretched Little Song,
For its Air Breath,
Was Still,
And Cold!

RESUME

Eagle in the Ashes.
Bricks 'n' Mortar Lay,
        Resume,

Crumble 'n' Ruin,
Blitzed are the Twisted shards,
Wood 'n' Nails Spat,
        Resume,

Ode to the Hammer.
And the Lathe,
A Carpenter Lathe,
Of this our Picture
        Lay.

Infant Holy,
Christ,
Is born,

With Golden Crowns 'n' Thistles,
Now your Stone has rolled away,
When Carols your Dance in Triumph,

Pray, Resume...!

THE GIFT

Having Been Pierced With Nails,
Clothed In Sorrows,
Is The Cup,
And The Bread,
The Gift,
Most Holy!!

A MOST JOYFUL OF PILGRIMS

Oh I Did Walk,
Where He Has Been,
For He Carried Me Then,
For I Was Lame,
And My Foot Was Soar,
So Through The Ancient Street We Did Wander,
Of Zion City Of Our God,
And So Those Sights And Sounds Were So
Intoxicating,
For I Remember It Well,
Together With Those Smells,
Of Old Jerusalem,

Oh Then Into The Desert He Spirited Me,
Feeling That awesome Heat,
This Most Joyful Of Pilgrims,
To See The Most Mystic Of Bedwyn People's,
                    With Caravan-A-Load,

Beneath Flowering Bush,
A- Waterside,
Then Travelling A-Far,
Disappear From Whence They Came,
Into Their Spoken Desert,

With Baggage Colour,
Under No-ones Command,

Oh Then I Found Myself,
Did I,
With My Lord,
Beside Still Waters Of The Jordan,
Where His Baptism had Take Place,
And So We Drunk A While,

Later My Lord Took Me To Calm Waters,
Did Its Aroma,
Smell Sweet,
Did Galilee,
Where Once My Lord,
Did Teach Men To Fish For Men,

And All At Once,
I Found Myself With Him,
In Such A Garden I Have Never Seen The Like Of Before,
For He Was The Second Adam,
My Lord,
Where He Did First Appear,
To Oh Sweet Mary,
The Magdalen,

And So I Asked A Question Of Him,
Before We Went Each To Our Own Separate Way,
And It Was This,
 Oh Then Where Do I Fit Into This?

>Memories Of Touring
The Holy Lands
November, '90

CHILDREN OF JERUSALEM

Children Of Jerusalem,
Look Always,
From Those Dark Satanic Mills,
Knowing That There Is A Brighter Tomorrow,
As Our Septic Isle She Is A Beauty,
Glistening In All Her Seasons,
For Don't Dwell On Shelves Of Empire Of History,
But Rather Shine And Live For This Your Day,
For The Chains Have Been Broken,
Broken In The Night,
You Are Freemen This Day,

For It Is Written,
Scribed In Stone,
Through The Spine Of This Wonderful Land,
Oh My Children,
For We Are The Orbiting Onion,
Toller-ant And Seeking Peace,
Then Go on,
Hand The Baton On,
To Those who Are Waving,
But Not Drowning,
Oh My People,

For This Is How We Shall Shine In The Morning, Oh My Children!!

CONFLICT BETWEEN COUSINS

Peace is the True Battle!

Israel And Her Arab Neighbours

JESUS CHRIST

Jesus Christ,
Christmas Is,
The Shepherds hillside visitation,

Come now Emanuel,
And bring your Dazzling Light,

Baptizing,
Carpenter,
With such Flame,
Be the anointed Nazarene,
Kissed 'n' Stripped,
For your Tangled Crown,

I must now know,
Did you choose and make Salvations
                                    Tree,

To Grow?
For if you did?
This is now such a Gospel

When Caravans and Kings,
Did Ride.

THE GOLAN

Wintery,
With All That Ice And Snow,
Here In The Heights,
Does It Blow,
The Golan Heights,

Have You Seen Nimrods Castle?
Watching,
Looking Over,
The Boarder Lands,
Of Conflict,
War,
And Pain,

Nimrod,
How I Shiver,
Your Spirit Is Certainly Alive And Well,
Brooding,
Stirring Up Old Malice And Hate!!!

The Golan
November 1990

GAZA

Oh Where Do We Go?
Where Do We Run?
For There Is No Where To Go,
For We Have No Money,
And We Have No Water,
For Please Help Us,
For Don't You See,
This Is The Great And Might Vengeance
                         Of Benny,
                             Benny!

THE WAR CASUALTY

War,

A Twelve Year Old,
An Orphan,
That Has Seen,
And Lost Everything,
What A Lot For A Child To See,
Now Beneath A Canvas Roof,
Caught In The Crossfire,

Of War!

ISRAEL'S CHILDREN

A Tree It Weeps,
As Does The Willow,
Tears,
For Its People,
For In Old Jerusalem Town,
David's Star Does Flutter,
Blue As It Colour,
In the Morning,
Just As Her Army Muster,
For Your Men Folk,
Wave Their Sad Eyed Tearful
                      Farewells,

To Loved Ones,
Uttering,
Tying Prayers On The Wind,
For With Kisses They Love,
Signeye,
Signeye!

AND THE DRAGON MADE WAR

And The Dragon Opened His Mouth,
And Smoke Came From The Mouth,
And The Dragon Breathed Fire,
For There Was Weeping And Gnashing Of Teeth,
                              Up On The Heights,

And So The Dragon Made War!

                                      Middle East
                                    Autumn '23 - '24
                                        A Year On

LOVE MOST FRANKED

Love Most Franked,
When Kind By The Hand,
Is Written On Yellow And Pink,
Dropping Through My Letter Box,
When Thoughts At Once Turn To You,
                    Perfumed One,

Of A Holiday Hill,
Where Waters Glimmered,
Banked In A Romance,
When Letters Travelled,
County Wide,
Being At Once First Class,
A Lick And A Stamp,
With Ones Kiss,
Brought Two Hearts Then,
                    Nearer,

My Love!!

DICTATORS

Dictators,

Are Usually Small Guys,
Jobs Worths,
Offering Some Kind Of Dream,
Banging A Fist On The Table,
Shouting,
Whilst Carrying A Gun,
Promising You The Earth,
With The Hand On The Trigger,

Then Comes Jack Boot And Hurt,
Whilst Democracy Flies From The Window,
Like The Dove,
Then Keep Watch From Your Tower!

THE ANGEL SHARE

The Angel Share,
Melts into the clear blue Sky,
And like the
Swallows are gone.

THE BLACK MADONNA

Crystal streams run,
Silver in their Fortune
With Alpine hurt,
When,
Ripples the Wind,
Song,
For Black is the Face,
Of our Lady Madonna,
          Sweet,

Does She Weep,
Tears,
Behind Her Bars,
Those wretched Bars,
In our begotten Chapel,
Of the Mountain,
          Far,

For a King has lost his Crown,
        Lost his Crown,
Oh Ebony wood,
Smile on me Michael!

                At The Church Of Częstochowa

SINS OF MAN

The Dark Hung As The Night,
Bleed Purple,
Of The Christ Cloud On Golgotha's Tree,
Was The Kiss,
Silently,
Of The Sins Of Man!

IN THESE LEAVES

What Has Become Of Us?
In The Leaves,
     Mum!

For The Leaves Bring Shadows,
To Our Day,
     Mum,

There Is No Warmth,
And Tenderness Of Heat,
         Mum!

In The Day Of Summer Sun,
         Mum,

Dreaming Of But Idol-ness,
         Mum!

OCTOBER 7TH

Hamas,

Came To Israel,

With An Attack,

To Snatch,

To Kidnap,

And To Kill,

Like Thief's In The Night,

Sparking,

Triggering War,

Awful War!

ANOTHER FORBIDDEN PLACE

The Midnight Hour,
Is Simply Another Forbidden Another
                    Place,

Just As The Fruit!

CANDY CANES AND CARNIVALS

In My Father's House,
It Is Full Of Nutcracker Dolls,
Ginger Bread Men,
And Toffee Apples,
With Helter Skelter Rides,
When The Fair Comes To Town,
For The Girl Is On The Trap-ease,

In My Father's House,
For There Are Shies,
And Rides,
For Some Are As Magical As Magical,
Like The Hall Of Mirrors,
Or Miss. Maggie's Table Of Cards,
Along With The Ball,
Seeing Our Future Journey's Way,
When Clowns Cause Chaos,
And Caroline Louise,
Well She's Sawn In Two,

For All This Happens,
Horses Dance On The Carousel,
And Still Others Well They Prefer The Wall Of Death,

With Candy Canes And Other Things,
For The Lights Are Bright Tonight,
In My Father's House.

INSOMNIA

Empty Is The Night,
As Insomnia,
With That Aimless Rolling,
Tossing 'n' Turning,
Restless,
Although The Covers Are Warm,

Restless Is The Night,
Like The Seas,
Guided By The Moon,
With The Tides,
         Restless,

As The Migrants,
Seeking A Home,
Refuge,
From Their World,
For Isn't This What Dreams Are Made Of?
Oh Again My Friend,
These Are The Life Sucking Seas
     Of Wretched Insomnia!

BELTANE

Shortening Nights,
Lighter Days,
Brighter Than Bright,
Is The Light,
Of Beltane,
With Fire,
With Flame,

All Consuming,
Is The Burning,
With Tongues Lapping,
At The Wicker,
Dance Then You Children
Around Your Pole Of May,
Making Merriment,

Between Equinox,
Come,
For The Sun Is Chasing Your Winter Away,
With Impressionist Colour,
Like A Cataract,
Water Flow,
Celebrate Then The Celtic's,
        Of Beltane!!

GRANDMA'S IMAGINATION

Take Locomotion Number One,
Through Her Garden Of Delights,
Of Flowered Fairy's Of Mosaic's And Magic,
Where The Skies Are Born Each Day Bluer Than Blue,
And The Juice Is Of The Colour Of The Sun,
                         An Amber Golden,

When The Fruits Of The Leaves,
Are Of Barley Sugar Candy.
Cast By The Wizards Of The Day,
When The Mirrored Bow Bowed His Head,
Glinting At The Unicorn,
To See The Old White Stag,
Dancing With The Young Lion,
                         There,

With The Hares In The Fields,
A-Plenty,
Whilst Grandma's Fertile Imagination Ran Riot,
Getting Drunk On Mysterious Giggle Water,
For In That Chaos Did Her Minor Bird Escape,
And Was Devoured By Kitty Well Forest,
To The Left Of The Three Witches Tree!!

MELANCHOLY FORTUNE

We Are All Melancholy Now,
For The Mists Hang Low,
Preventing The Dawn From Shinning,
For We Do Not Have The Happiness,
That Moved About Us,
Of Yester Year,
For There Is No Joy,

Sad That It Is,
No Laugh,
No Smile,
For She Has Been Taken From Us,
By Wind And Sail,
For The Mists Have Swallowed Her,
Taking Her Sweet Love,
Like Yester Years,
        Roses!

                              Mother

THE PAST MASTER

The Past Is A Big Country,
Although I Did Not Expect It To Take Me,
So Far Back In My Memory!!

EYES OF MINE

Eyes See Do Mine,

Observing,

With This Pen Of Mine!!

WAY OUT MAN

The End Is The Beginning,
When Launching A Far Out Star Ship,
                                                Man,
Is The Tattoo,
Orange,
Over The Jungle Girl,

Jumping Through Rings Of Juice Smokin'
When Swallowing That Lucy,
In A Wired Wave Of COLOUR,

For It Is,
Just,
Ours To Gain Man,
Peace And Love!!

                              A Kaleidoscope Of Sixties

THE ROBIN

Heralding In The Season,
Breasted And Scarlet,
With Your Brown Backed -Wing,
Now On every Other Little Card,
Is This Territory Bird,
Chirping,
Greater Than He Is?

DANK

Dank,
Quite Warm,
It Gets In My Bone,
I Loathe It,
You Know,
The Damp,
An' So I Shiver,
With Aching,
Has Somebody Put A Spell On Me?

HIBERNATION

Autumn,
Coloured Leaves,
In Showers 'n' Pull-eds,
When Kicking At The Leaves,
I Quite Like It,
For Closing In,
When Falling Back,
To Hunker down,
Whilst Waiting For The Magical Time,
Around Our Fire,
Oh To Sleep,
To Sleep,
Now!!

FRESH MORNING AIR

Fresh Morning Air,
Oh So Clear,
It's A New Day,
Breathe It,
You Can Almost Taste It,
            Then,

Engage With It,
And Play Your Part,
For Its A Privilege,
My Friend,
    Then,

Don't Waste Your Time,
For Be At Peace,
        Then,

In The Garden!!

I AM LISTENING

If You Should Ask Me,
What I am Doing Here?
I am Listening,
I am Waiting,
Whether It Is To The Winds In The Trees,
Or The Tides,
They Shall Speak The Voice Of God,
                          Here,
For I Have Belonging,
           Here,
For Beneath The Stars There Is Mind-fullness,

Just As God Is On The Shores,
Come The New Dawn,
I Have Peace,
Perfect Peace,
Here,
My Friend,
Just As The Leaves Do Blow,
In The Fall!

WONDER HOLE

OH TAKE THE RED PEN,
AND I WILL SHOW YOU,
HOW DEEP THE WONDER HOLE IS!!

LAYER YOUR DEW FALL

Layer Your Dew Fall,
     Oh Magic One,

For The Earth Is Thick
With Sparklin' Diamonds,
             Child,

After The Freezing Frosted Night,
Our Young Jack Danced His Way,

And Cast A Spell On Our Garden,
                So!!

FISH 'N' CHIPS

Fish 'N' Chips,
And Eating,
Fish 'N' Chips,
With Vinegar,
And Your Salts,
Are Ones Finger,
All Wrapped Up,
In Yesterdays News,
On The Top Of A Number Ten Bus,
There's A View To Be Had,
My Lad,

Whilst I Wish That I Had,
Some Ketchup,
My Lad!!

COLOURED LIKE RAIN

Our Little Life Is Nothing More Than Dreams Are Made Of,
Wrote Our Bard,

        Mother,

When One Considers Of Our Pain,

Through The Winds On The Mind,

        'COLOURERED'

Like The Little Children's Shower Of Rain,

Are Missals,

Of Bent Up Anger!

WEBS

Have You Seen The Webs,
Of Autumn Leaves?

That Hang,
For The Spider Has Spun,
                       Webs,

Of Golden Brown,
In The Dew Drop And Rain,

Defining Gravity,
The Spider Climbs And Spins,

His Trap To Snare,
Our Gate Post And Gutter,

Weaving,
For It Was The Time Of Year,

Just Then Our Spider Crawled Out Of The Wood Pile,
Seeking Warmer Climbs In Doors My Love!

THE OLD WHEEL HOUSE

Standing Alone,
Set By The Sea,
Against The Weather,
Man Could Be,
Is The Old Wheel House,
Of The Cornish Mine,
Going Deep Beneath The Sea,
For Worthy Ore,
         Man And Boy,

For The Wheel House,
Now Topples,
Echoing Stacks Of Tumblin' Ruin,
Spread To The Winds,
Like Wings Of Time,
Your Singin' Compass Tells,
Herned With Pick 'N' Shuvell,
Were The Pittans Of Chips You Made,

Cousin Jack!!

TWO FACES
(Middle East Conflict)

Grey Ashen Faces,

White With Death,

White With Dust,

In Rubble Of Ruin,

Children Caught,

Screaming,

Bewildered,

Along With The Poor,

Whoever They Are?

Israel And Lebanon Are Warring!

HOMELESSNESS

ROOTLESS,

IS HOMELESSNESS,

IS A STIGMA,

DARK!

HOMELESS ANGEL

Angels at Night,
Angels in the Shadows,
Injecting themselves,
Begging on the Side Walk,
Begging for a Meal,
Laying their Head on a Cardboard Pillow,
                            Discarded as they,

By a Society that is!
That has no Answers,
In Town and Country Arches,
Beneath Subway Lines,
And Department Stores,
Tells a different Story other than The Theatre
Lands,   Serviced by Colour,

These Angels 'n' Folk,
Are befriended with Blood and Thunder,
A Testimony to did you receive Mary,
Wingless Bird that you,
With your ragged Dress 'n' wind blown Hair,
Go to your Garden,
Rather than the Neon Shadows,
Of Darkness 'n' Harm!

AGGI'S GONE

Aggi's gone
Now the Pavements bear,
In the cold night Air,
Where Aggi slept,
Between board 'n' blanket,
In the cold night Air,
                    Where?
There!
In Boutport Street,
Where?

Says, the Worshipful flowers,
There!

Now Aigg's gone,
What does anyone care?
Now he's Gone,
Gone to God,
Fucking God,
With Angels 'n' Stars,

Where? There!
In the cold night Air.

                          Alan 'Aggi' Aageson 54

DARTMOOR PRISON

Haunted Walls,
Enclosing,
Like The Mists,
Built From Granite,
Grey 'N' Damp,
Built By The French,
Oh So Long Ago,
Like This Monster,
Rolling In,

Upon The Unforgiving Moor,
For Themselves,
Toiling Sweatin' Hard,
For Their Gruel,
Which Surrounded Them,
And Encaged Them,

For The Trouble Was,
The Governor, Prisoners,
Were All Doing Bird Together,
Under Such Ugly Beautiful Weather!

A NOTE TO MR. MAGPIE

Hi! Mr. Magpie,
How's Your Wife?
For You Know,
That I Know,
PC 380 Is Lookin' For You,
Don't You Know,

For You Stole Those Twinklin' Jewels So,
For Your Nest,
To Line,
Didn't You?
And So PC 380 Will Question You,

And A Rest You,
Clipping Those Wings,
And So You Won't Go Be Able To Go To The
Greenwood So!!

SOLITUTUED IS

Solitutued Is,
Not Loneliness,

Solitutued Is,
Very Important,

Solitutued Is,
Left To You To Find Your Own Space,

Solitutued Is,
Thought Of As A Negative Thing,

Solitutued Is,
Very Much A Privilege,

Solitutued Is,
Excellent If One As It?

Solitutued Is,
Precious If A Person As It?

MUSING ON BOOKS

Go On,
Read A Book,
A Precious Book,
Emerse Yourself,
Delve Into Its Contents,
Line By Line,
Turning Pages,
    Quietly,

Of Chapter And Verse,
Of History And Character,
Be A Storyteller,
A Conjurer Of The Word,
Whether It Be History Or Poetry,
Let It Jump Out At You,

All Is But A Library,
Hold It To Ones Heart,
Be A Storyteller,
For One Book,
Does Not Make A Library,
        My Child!

VERITY

Verity,

She Stands On The Pier,
Raising Her Sword,
High,

Heavy Wild Child,
Coiled Deep Inside Her,
                See,

Bearing Her Load,
With Motherhood Soon To Be,
Proud For All To See,

Naked Is Your Lady,
Oh Damien
At The Harbour,
For Comb,

In All The Comings,
An' Goings,
She Was Sculpted From Clay,
For Man And Man Alone,
Will Be,

Does She Stand,
Curved
Tall With Feminity.

> Ilfracome
> North Devon

BULL POINT LIGHT

Wined Your Journeys way,
Through A Devon Lane,
Cast Your Pebble Out,
See it Ripple,
A-Far,
From A Shore,
To Who Knows Who?

When The Light Stand Tall,
And White,
Broad Is Its Beam Of Light,
When Its Fog Horn Does Blow,
Sounding The Channel Sheer,
                          Clear,

Of The Bristol Channel!

                                  North Devon

THE BOGEYMAN

There Is No Other Villain,
Other Than Addiction Itself,
Appearing Like The Bogeyman's
                             Face,

Appearing Out From Behind The Closet,
                         Creaking Doors!

THE PRINT ROOM

Deep In The Print Room,
Surrounded By Ink Paper,
Awear Of Odders 'n' Machines,
I Gazed At My Bosses,
In Longing And Wonder,
At Their Cars,
Their Jags,
The Quality Fords,

In How They Dressed,
In Sharpe Suited Cloth,
Having Dinning Out,
On The Company,
And There Was I,
Lame With Hopes And Dreams,
Receiving Little,
For Those Hours,
Just Getting Filthy,

Looking Out Onto The Window,
On My Dreams,
Buried In Reams,
And Yet More Reams,
Until One Sunny Day,

I Awoke And Was Going To Have My Way,
For So I told The Galloping Major,
To Take His Job And Shove It!!!

                                                              Shaplands
                                                              1979-85

MUSING ON THOSE LONG SUMMER DAYS
(To The Chaddiford Lane Gane, 1972-77)

Oh Once Everything Flew,
In Those Long Far Days,
Since,
We   Had Joy,
Just As The Swallows,
For Then We Grew,
Up And Away,
For Some Of Us Even Had Children
                              Then,

And Before We Knew It,
The Melancholic Winter Came,
The Summer Had Lost Its Shine,
Once We No Longer Ran,
Or Skipped In Our Mischievous Gangs,
For Some Of Us Ached Now With Pains,
          A-Plenty Coming Our Way,

For Even Then Some Still Had,
Cataracts Done,
Knew Hips,
And Those Pacemakers Fitted,
When Others Had Fallen A Sleep,

Deep To Their Rest,
    Old Friends,

Do You Remember?

SOMERS FALL

Autumn day, harvest, Autumn gold,
Taste,
Furnished burnished beech bronze,
Tinted in the shadow lands,
Mellow mists low where pleasant waters flow.

Reminiscences, toast of a Puritan past,
In hostelries now, built as stations then.
Colour my memory with your New Model Army.
A fragment lost like Somers Past.

Journey on to Dulverton, and the sound of the distant rut
Where the old clapper Bridge still stands to serve and to span,
The Barle,
Trippers now.

Though at the Trigg spot, he light fades,
Way like my view, like my words running,
Like the river runs to the Sea, to the Sea.

First Poem Published
Written At The White Horse Exford

SOMER PEOPLE

The Morris Men Dance,
      When,

To the Dominion of the Somer People,
Wassailing,
In the Orchards of Life,
      Old Life,
Spills,

Telling of Legends,
And Dragons,
      When,

Before Our new Faith,
Came planted,
      A Tree,

When At Glastonbury,
In Prayer My Fellow,
For Knights Were Good,
And Followers Of The Way,

Dances you Morris Men,
For Red are the Deer,

And Golden the Cheese!

When Time is Passing,
In this Dominion that is?

You that are,
The Mysterious People,
             That are,

Somer!

RED EYES
(To A Nephew)

Red Eyed,
Red Hair,
Living In Old Shanghai,
High In The Air,
Seeing All That Glistens,
        And Dazzles,

You've Been Taken In,
Rattling Up The Dollars,
Rather Than China!

AND WITH IT AUTUMN COMES

And With It Autumn Comes,
Growing Darkness,
Snap Crackle And Fire,
With Trick Or Treater,
Burning Their Farage,
With Witches Out Tonight,
Sendin' Ghostly Shivers,
Through With The Winds,
For The Spirits Are Out Tonight,
Up Grave Yards Hollow,
For A Part From The Season It Is But A
                Melancholy Season,

In This A Very Dreary Day,
It Also Has A Sparkly Attitude!

WIND

Wind,
It Wafts Up Taw Vale,
All The Day Long,
Under Those Arches,
Bring The Tide In,
For The Season Of Man,
And Already The Bell Is A-tollin'
                    Tollin'!

SHATTERED LIVES

Shattered Lives,
Are As Castles,
Ruins In Themselves,
Little Sister!!

AUTISM

Address Your Mask,
Then You Shall Be Who You Are,
In Your Natural State,
For I Know You Long To Do So,
For Then You Shall Do As You Please,
Within This The Garden Of Delights,
I Have Created For You,
         My Child!

GREAT UNCLE RONALD AND HIS COMBINATION

Great Uncle Ronald,
Was Married To Winifred,
Or My Winnie Has He Called Her,
And They Came From The North,
Riding The Roads,
They Both Rode And Travelled The Roads,
                                            Wildly,

On An Old Military Combination,
For It Spluttered And Flew,
Faster Than Fast,
Eating Up The Tarmac,
Under Canopy's Of Colour,
For One Morning They Even Raced
    And Beat The Flying Scotsman,

For That Was Something,
Riding A Combination,
With Flying Helmets On,
And Googles Down,
When Buster Was Barking Loudly,

For Buster Was Winnie's Dog,
He Was, He Was,

Whilst Great Uncle Ronald Had His Combination,
Cider And Snuff,
For There Were Those Who Called Him,
A Cider And Snuff Man,

As A French Polisher,
Called Him Nothing But A Cider And Snuff Man,
And Winifred Herself She Liked A Bloody Mary,
I'm Telling You There Was Nothing So Funny,
As The Three Of Them Travelling On The Open Road,
When They Were Having A Northern Jolly A Bit Tipsy Like!!

THE FLOWERS

The Flowers Are Perfect,
In The Garden,
      Now,

Oh Sweet Mumma,
Mute To Our World,
In The Stillness.

THE LEPER'S LANE END

There Will Be Trouble,
A Still Voice Uttered,

And So Blood And Disaster,
Came To The Beautiful Game,
In A Cush Of Death,
To The Leper's Lane End,

 Anger From Mouths Of Relatives,
Spoke Ever Louder In Courtroom Battles,
Remembered When Poignant Was The Word,
                                        Played,

Listed Loved Ones,
Now,
And So The Cathedral Sings!!

                                        South Yorkshire
                                        15th April 1989

THE TREES

Rings Of Age,
The Ancient Tree,
Give A Pleasant Smell,
        An Odder,

As They In Hale,
And Exhale,
With Moss Gathering At Their Heels,

Standing In Union.
Often As A Couple,
With Roots Running Deep,
          Beneath,

Binding,

Oh Listen To The Trees,
Ear Them Talk,
Those Swaying Leaves,
Hark Now To The Birds,
Singing Sweet Songs,

Darting,
Darting From Tree To Tree,

Both Woodpecker And Jay,
To Name But Two,
In The Canopy,

For The Trees Of The Forest,
Do Not Have Voices As We,
         My Dear!!

MUSING ON THE LOOKING GLASS

For Once I Did Walk Those Carpets Of Purple,
When Major The Minor Was Near,
        With His Chatter,

And I Did Play On Nanna More's Scales,
        For Once I Was A Child Then,

When A Magpie Circled,
For Poetry Ran Through My Veins,
With Seven Inch Disc's Shaping My Dreams,
Then When Old Schools Mates Ran Fast,
Into Those Thankless Jobs,
For Then The Old School Gates Were Closed
                Unto Them,

And So We Who Are Left,
While Away The Hours,
And Reflect,
On What Might Have Been,

My Good Friend,
Friend,
Oh Friend You Were,
        You Were!

WARDROBE TALK

Oh Love Is A Ritual,
When In The Last Kiss Given,
However Short The Conversation Given,
For David Lays Here Now,
The Music Man,
Laying With His Mother,

For Also I am Reading Normans Dates,
Has He Been Really Gone That Long?
Like You Old Friend,
Hanging Like Memories,
As Clothing At The Back Of Some Wardrobe!

LIBERTY AT PEGASUS BRIDGE
(THE EIGHTIETH ANNIVERSARY OF D. DAY
6-6-2024)

We Shall Always Remember Them,
Those Brave Young Men,
Who Appeared In Our Normandy Sky,
And Left On Foot,
Changing Our Destiny,
Forever And A Day,
For We Are Free,
For We Have The Liberty,
Via Liberty!!!

FELL!
(Remembering D. Day - 80 Years On)

He's Dead,
I'm Crippled,
We're Alive,
That's The Consequences Of War,

And Now Old Pal,
We're Off To Normandy,
To Remember You Who Fell!

THE WOMAN OF WOE

Oh This Is The Tale,
Of The Woman Of A Woman,
Wearing Her Hurt Like Clothing,
In This A Sorrowful Tale,
For She Paces Out The Yard,
Face To The Ground,
Striding Out The Mile,
      Twice Daily,

Each And Every Day,
For There Are Two Of Them,
Seats I Mean,
A Mile A Mile A Part Or So,
She Mourns Her Son,
By Sitting,
Grieving,
And Moving On,
With A Little Prayer,

She Needs To Let Go,
The Woman Of Woe,
But She Will Always Remember,
Her Beloved,
Much Mist Son,

Although She Needs To Let Go,

This Woman of Woe,
Bearing Aloud Of Woe,
Something Has Bound Her,
Something Holds Her,
But I Can't Help Her,
She Needs To Break Those Chains,
                        That Hold,

In The Night,
Then She Shall See The Light!!

MUSE ON A LOSS

Oh Once I Went To Church,
It's True,
So Long Long Ago,
When The Swallows Smiled On Me,

That Was Before The Fire Consumed My Son,
A Tuneful,
Happy Boy,

For I Was Baptised Into The House Of Our Lord,
It's True
But Church Is Not For Me Anymore,
Since That Wretched Fire,
Killed My One And Only Beloved Son,

For Oh I Have Prayed, And Asked Why?
He Was Taken,

For Even The Queen Of Heaven,
Is Silent On Such A Matter,
Yet She Was The Mother To Our Lord,
Then Why Should I Go To Church?
When There Is No Answer Forth Coming?
From These Echoing Walls That Surround Me!

BUDE

Crumpled Sheets,
And a weary Head,
Talking of dreams 'n' Pillow Sleep,
Listening to the Breakers Break,
                      And Roll,
You carry Me Gull,
There as You go,
Down over Crooklets,
And Summerleaze Way,
To Your Crashin' Seas 'n' Barrow Rock,
                      Barrow Rock,
Much Painted,
Now,
Others Turn Pages,
As you Scrounge!
Both Pasty, Chip and Ice,

Whilst others play their Venture Games,
Being Skipper and Crew,
All the day long,
The Bell Gongs,
Gongs, at St. Michaels,
And Gongs,

Whilst in your town,
Tills do Roll,
Another sale is made,
For The Ark Angel spreads his Wings,
Together with your Falcon,
Methodists do Sing,
Then Your Lucky Kiss is made,

What a Break!
Around The Globe,
Your happy, happy Globe.

SEWERS OF LIFE

Oh Hang Out The Washing,
Mrs. Jones,

See The Folks Are Dirty.
One To Another,

In All Their Ways,
One To Another,

In The Langaue That They Use,
One To Another,

Neigbour Verses Neighbour,
Among Those Tenement Blocks,

For All That's Happening Is The Poor Are
Getting Poorer,
And The Rich Are Getting Richer,

This Was Not Meant To Happen Mrs. Jones,
Ole Mr. Basil Jet Would Be Ashamed Of You!

GRAFFITI POEM

Graffiti Poems are in my Heart,
If you don't like this,
Take a look at what the Tories,
Are doing.

SPIRIT MOOR

And Aged Song,
Buzzard, Hare,
And Curlew Fly,
Spirit Of Our Great Moor,
Chiselled Winds,
      Loom,

And Pixie Progress,
Blessed,
Streams cross Like Ribbons Of Water,
Crystal,
With Oreo In Their Flow,

Voices Fury,
Coloured Face Of Purple Heather,
Yellow Gorse,
And Fern Of Green,
Grey In Mists and Granite,
           Artistic,

Ponies Bray,
Walls Are Dry stone,
Durra Wood,
And Paint Oh Spirit Moor!

GREYSTONE MEMORIES

A Dartmoor walk,
Goes a-wanderin',
To Greystone,
Hearing Echo's,
Through its Walls,
Of People's past,
Caught in the Snows,
Of Petroc's Bells,

Stepping out a Jar to many,
There the Lost Cord,
Was heard,
At Castles Keep,
A-Hunting, We did go,
Yonder Widgery,
At Lydford Town,
Where the blizzard wind,
Does rise 'n' howl,
Oh hanging Judge,
Forgetting not,
        "Dear Lionel"

Shepherd of your Sheep,
For a Dartmoor walk,

Goes a-wanderin'
Amid the purple heather,
Then takes my seat,
With a Cockade in my heart,
Of sweet Reminiscences,
For kissing Mary Jane neath the Mistletoe!!
        Carolling on, first Footing,

Into that New year.

                Appears In Hidden Paths

SPIRITS HAVING FLOWN

It Happened On a Tuesday,
              Then,

When Me And My Brother,
Took a Journey,
            Then,

To Where Our Lyd Would Flow,
Rapid 'n' Deep,
Knowing Something Was Good,
                    There,

Although When We Arrived,
Did Not a Soul Exist,
But Echoing Walls,
And Boyhood Haunts,
          Of Old,

                  Were Greystones,
                      Granite,

Just As The Will Of The Wisp,
Like Though Spirits That Had Flown,
Laughin' And Chucklin',

Those Ribbons Of Waters,
That Sang On Those Moor,
     With Heavens Gaze,

That Had Conceived Them So,
Long Since - In Days Ago,

And So We Raised Our Glasses,
Not Once But Twice,
     To Many,
There,

At Castles Keep,
To Bygone Spirits,
Having Flown,

Although Before We Turned,
To Say,
   'Farewell'

We Visited The Path,
   Of The Yew,

To Read The Names,
Of Those We Knew,
Etched In Colourless Grey,

Like The Moor
That Had Conceived Them So,

And So If We Were To Return,
That Same Way?
Only Those Spirits Would Know,
For The Journey was Long,
And Tiresome,
      Then,

And Alas Dear Brother,
I Soon Came To The Conclusion That Their
Chapter Had Ended,
And Therefore We Do Not Belong Here
Anymore,
For Those Spirits In Which We Had Known,
                          Had Flown!

                Platinum Jubilee Week

MOOR AT HOME

I Feel Moor At Home
              Here,

It's Strange,
It Must Be In The Genes,
I Suppose,

With The Carpets Of Purple,
And Crossed By Giggling Crystal Ribbons Of Ores,
Are These Brooding Tors,

Do You Know,
I Feel Moor At Home
              Here,

Than In Any Other Place!!

                                      Lydford
                                      Devon

TIDES

Our Tides Are High,
Political,
    Like,

Beneath The Arches!

TOO PC

There Isn't Any Love,
Any More,
You Can't Look At Somebody,
And Give Them A Smile,
                No,

That Would Be Wrong,
Everyone Is Too PC,
Caught In Their Own Little Diary Of Doin's,
And Worries,
Lost In A Private Bubble Of Woe,

There Isn't Any Love,
Anymore,

                !!True!!

AGREE

Just Agree With Ones Wife,
Boys!!

A SHOT OF WORDS

An Addict Cries,

Oh Give Me A Shot Of Words,
                        Sister,

With Your Needle,
There,

I Wanna It,
I Fuckin' Need It,
Words I Mean,
Running Through My Bloody Veins,

I Wanna Live In Another Person,
For Its Intoxicating,
 As A Magician,
A Wizard Most Spell Binding,

For They Won't Know,
The Reader,
All Caught Up In A Web Of Words,
                Glorious Words!!

LANG DALE MUSE

From Troutbeck
Did a Bus we Ride,

Brings Autumn sickle,
Harvest Wind,
Drinking,
Amber Nectar,
With Mine Eye,
Sees the Hardwick,
On your Fell

Whilst cruel is this month,
October now,
In colours resplendent,
Cold,
Helicopters fall,
To children's Playground antics
                      Known,

Wistful Time,
Of green undoing,
Spoken in Face of Teal,
Are Lang Dales,
Muse,

Below,
When crossing Her mirrored
Pond,
Through Golden mists of Celestial
                            Core,

And did Jemima come all at once running
Down the hill,
Way from Top Hill Farm?
And Mr. Todd.

DAD

Dad you taught me to walk,
            To walk,

Alongside Soldiers that marched,
In Tunic's Red,
In Tunic's Red,
With mirrored feet,
And Bear Skin black,
Do they shine,

You taught me to walk,
    Taught me to walk,

First by the left,
And then the right,
Marching,
Marching,
Up Windsor Great Hill,
Like Soldiers on Parade,
Like Soldiers on Parade,

Dad you taught me to Walk,
            To walk,

You did!
You did!
All that time ago,
 Time ago!

LAST KISS
(A Mothers Kiss - Leaving Harbour)

When Did She last Kiss me?
In the Car Park,
She last Kissed me,
So long, long, ago,
In the Days of Wine,
      And Roses,

She Kissed me,
The Piano Plays,
Now She Sits,
With quiet Hands,
And Distant Eye,
Backward Stepping,

When Did She last Kiss me?
In the Car Park,
She Kissed me,
So long, long, ago.
The Piano Plays.

      This Took Place at a Garden Centre

THE PIANO

The Piano Echo's Sad Memories,
                              Now,

Of Times When Were Of Joy,
And Fines Tunes 'n' Songs Were Played,

Although It Seems To Be Forgotten,
Way Laid In Dust,
Knowing I Suppose The End Must Be Soon,

Etched Out,
Until It To Will Be Escorted Out,
Like Its Owner!

                    And My Mother Played

ALONG THE GRANITE WAY
(A Lydford Rabble)

To Set The Scene,
Caught Up Was I,
In My Muse,
I Scrabbled Up There,
Alongside Widgery,
And His Golden Cross Of Jubilee,

 Once There,
I Could Be Free,
With Blessing My Friend,
With Black Faced,
And Those Five Pointers,
On A Carpet Of Purple,

Walking 'n' Wandering,
As I Did,
Between The Tors,
And Moors,
Of Granite Walls,
Through The Woodland,
      Of Fungi,

And Moss,

WITCHCRAFT

wicker,

witchcraft!

VIKING QUEEN

Helen,
Like Glass,
From Across The Sea,
The Dane,
      Reign In Me,

Oh Paint You A Picture,
Mists Of Time,
Rolling,
When Shores,
The Invader,

The Viking Sail,
You Queen,
She Comes,
Stepping,
Does The Fearful
      Warrior!

HALO MARY ON A SUNDAY

Halo Mary,
I'm Fond Of You,
Read Me Through,
Painted Lady
Approaching Me There,
In The Garden,
        Then,

I Thank You,
Clothed In Catholic Crimson,
Wearing Your Hairs In Curlers,
                      Then,

Smoking Your Ciggie,
Oh Now Dressed In A Thousand Windows,
                            Magdalen,

For She Believed She Was With The Gardener,
So Our Bible Tells,
Oh Knelt This Harlot Of Perfect Gold,
Having So Many Men Before,
Living In A Graffiti World Before,
Of Needles And Pins A-,
With Prayer And Petition,

For She Was The First To Meet Her Lord,
Running,
Running,
To Tell Those Fisher Folk,
From There Shimmering Sea,
Of Many Colours,
        Loud,

Halo Mary,
    Now!!

A CLOUD

There Is A Cloud Over My Sun.

SATAN'S APPROACH

Solemnly,
Solemnly,

I went to the Beach,
Down to the Beach,
Tangled in its Weed,
Where the Crows Nests are,
In Dereliction,
In Dereliction,
To Stir the Waters,
Grey,
And Green,
Dragging My Chains,

Was this Lame Man Walking,
Lost in the Swim,
Broad Foot,
And Crow Foot,
The Gulls Squawked,

Loosing My Innocence's,
For Satan had greeted Me,
That Same Morning,
Beguiling and Smiling,

Sifting Me in Winters Approach,
Dragging My Chains Behind,
Dragging My Chains Behind,
Captivating like Some Magician,
                Or Prince,

Conjuring,
Running on the Tide,
Time and Tide,
Riding his Great Leviathan,
In Worlds of Aching Groaning Mists,
                He Was to Laugh,
                    Laugh!!

Humorously,
PWUCKING Man's Desire,
Of Lie and Hate,
Pure Hate!
Making Waves,
      Waves,

Full of Face,
Was The Clown,
Was The Clown!

RAFAEL'S SENTIMENT

I Have seen,

Rafael,

Rafael,

In the Corner,

In the Corner,

Sayin',

It'll be alright!

It'll be alright!

A TAKE ON THE NATIVITY
(A Poem For The Christmas Season)

Huddled,
Refugees Gather,
For There Is A Mother,
A Virgin,
Get Your Head Around That?

For I Am Their Christmas Tree,
Bowed Low,
Heavy With Sin,
For They Shall Use Me,
To Crucify My Lord,
The Powers That Be,

And There Are Shepherds,
Ever So Humble,
Really Humble,
In Their Dirt,
Employed By The Temple,

And There Are Said To Be Kings,
Following A Mysterious Light,
Coming With Caravans Of Camels,

Though None Of This Makes Much Sense,
Just To Visit A Babe?
And A Baby Boy,
      At That,

For The Nutcracker is Dancing Still,
                             On,
                     And On!

WHEN NEPHEW AND UNCLE TRAVEL
(Jesus And Joseph Of Arimathea Come Walking)

Shadow On The Wall.
Follow Me,
And Does Not Let Go,
When I Thought,
The Chains Had Been Broken,
        In The Night,

When Two Come A-Travelling,
So To I Rest At Your Alter,
Laden With Backie,
And Bread,
For Boy I Need To Drink Your Blood,

Oh Uncle Planted Your Staff,
Who Travelled Well,
And A-Far,
Through Arthur's Mystic Land Of Ore's
Travelling To Glastonbury,
Oh Once Did You Tor,
Boy From A-Far!

THE GREATEST STORY EVER TOLD
(The Gospel Short Cut - Poem)

Born In A Cavern,

Escaped Into Egypt,

Found In The Temple,

He Had Fishermen As Friends,

He Feed The Five Thousand,

With Loaves And Fishes,

For He Was The Carpenter,

Raising A Friend From The Dead,

Later Causing An Up Roar In The Temple,

What A To Do That Was,

For He Was Later Hung And Killed On A Tree,

Three Days Later A Harlot Found Him In The Garden,

And So She Ran To Tell His Friends.

For He Then Met Them And Told Them To Go Into All The World,

And Then He Vanished From their Sight,

With The Promise Of Coming Again!!

LUCIAN CAROL

Old World,
Pagan night,
Bringer of light,
Joined in festive celebration,
White berry,
Blood flow,
Life giving,
Pretty Lucia,
Come Children,
Dance with chocolate,
And Ginger bread Men,
In Stockin's and feet,
Down history street.

RITES

My Father comes to me,
                Risen,

In Confession,
Does,
He pray,
      Comforting!

This Sinner Man,
Does,
My Father come to me,
Pierced are his blooded hands
That Pour,
Together with those Blistered Feet,
                            Offering,
Offering,
Bread,
And Wine,
New Wine,

Crowned in Living Water,
Twisted in Thorns,
Once from the Rock of
                Moses,

Came his Rosary,
His Rosary,
St. Peter.

                    Dedicated to Father Philip

LYDIA
(Taken From The Bible)

Oh Lydia,
Lydia,

You Are But A Follower Of The Christ,
For You Are A Rich Woman,
Dying,
Selling Your Cloth,
A Merchant,
Simply A Head Of The Game,
With Skin And Hair Like Silk,

Oh Lydia,
Lydia,
My Dearest Lydia.

MARTHA'S POEM

I Have Often Wonder whether Or Not Martha
Felt Embarrassed,
To Be Corrected By Her Brothers Friend,
                                        Jesus?

Well Wouldn't You?
When Her Sister Was Commended,
By The Very Same Friend,
                              Jesus,

Although They Were Both Very Much Delighted,
When That Same Jesus,
Raised Their Brother Lazarus From The Dead,
And What A To Do,
That Was?

After All News Soon Travels,
For The Man Who Was Dead,
Was Now Very Much Alive,
And Well,
What A Sight For Soar Eyes That Must have
Been?

For He Came Out Of The Tomb,

He Did,
Wasn't Lazarus Lucky To Have Such A Friend?
My Dear!

WHEN IN BROAD LAND
(A Norfolk Delight)

Genteel Eyes of brown,
Are like deep pools,
When in Broad Land,
The Sails turn,
And the Greab She is nesting,
        Among the Reed,

When in Broad Land,
The little Children are Crabbing,
At Cromer,
Echo's the sound of the Fun Fair,
                Behind,

When in Broad Land,
As the Canary's play on,
So to do the Pilgrims throng,
And seek Bread,
Amid the Cloisters,
Of the Cathedral Church of The Trinity,

When in Broad Land.

THE DRAGONS AT THE DOOR

The Dragons At The Door,
Red With Rage,
From The East,
Now Arthur Has Drawn His Sword,
                  Excalibur,

And Merlin Mutters To Gaia,
When The Knights,
Have All Took Fright,
To The Crusades,
They've Gone,
Dear Guinevere,

For Your Chuff Is No Longer Insight,
My Dear,
When The Dragons At The Door,
Oh Sweet, Sweet,
        Avalon!

WISTMAN'S

Have You Seen The Ghost Bears At Play?
                        Grand As It Is,

For Some Say That It Is Haunted,
Deep Within Wistman's Wood,
Down Near The Silver Streams,
A-Rushing,
A-Rushing,
For Time Waits For No Man,

Where Merlin Walked,
With The Golden Griffin,
And The Unicorn Danced,

Deep Within Wistman's Wood,
Where The Fairies Are,
Flying High On Gossamer Wings,
For Its A Sight To Be Seen,
Telling This Tale Of Gossamer Wings,

And The Love Owl She Hoots,
Heralding In The Great White Stag,
Of The Wood,
As He Comes,

Beneath The Dark Sky Night,
When Stars Are Shinning Bright,
Upon Wistman's Ancient Wood,
Gnarled So,
Of Craft Of Long Ago,
Running Through The Veins Of Old Darty Moor!

                                        Wistman's Wood
                                               Dartmoor

SIMPLY TED

Sylvia Dearest,
      Nothing Is For Free,
      Everything Is Paid For!!

Yours Always Ted.

                              Ted Hughes

LETTER TO GRETA

Tinder Dry,
Tinder Keg,
The Earth It Burns,
With Flaming Fire,
She Is,
She Is,

With All Manner Of Political Conflict,
Of War And Famine,
For Famine Is Used As A Weapon,
You Know,
You Know,

So Greta,
Young As You Are,
You Might As Well Hold Your Hands Up,
And Amit For There Is Nothing You Or I Can Do Now,

The Oceans Are Rising,
The Pooler Caps Are Melting,
Melting,
Spinning Beyond Man's Control,
For everything Has Its Season,

My Love,
Even Our Beautiful,
Beautiful World!

Greta Thunberg

POSH
(Arm Chair Travel With The Telly)

When You Sleep,
Do You Weave Fairytales,
Into Your Dreams?
Spun With Silver Threads,
From The Silk Worms,
          There,

Oh India,
India,

Mighty Brahmaputra,
Whilst His Old Friend Ganesha,
Just Observed Like The Meandering River,
Had Seen It All Before,
For Even The Dolphins,
Are Drunk On Assam Tea,
Listening To Colonial Voices,
          There,

Taking Tiffin,
In Their Bungalows,
Whilst Speaking Of Hilda,
Lost In Deepest Surry,

It Was Then,
The Tiger Stirred From His Sleep,
Just As The Monks A-Rise,
Bathing Themselves In The Life Giver.

IN THE GARDEN OF ENGLAND

Winter Waning,
With Snow Drops And Daffodils,
In Orchards Of Hops,
In The Garden Of England,
A Genteel Paradise,
Where Canterbury Tales are A-Spoken,
And Bells Chime This Easter Morn,
For Even St. Augustine Stepped This Way,

And Dickens Was Still Very Much Alive,
What With The Dickens Festival,
Down Rochester Way,
Along The Medway,
Flowing Timeless To Meet Our Sink Ports,
Then Catch A Whiff Of Sea Breezes Blown,
At Broadstairs And Whitstable,
There We'll Taste Oysters,

For Taking A Ticket To Ride,
The Dim Church Line,
For The Kaiser And His Merry Men,
Never Did Make It To This Our Septic Isle,
And That's Why We're Still Free,
                    My Dear!

THAT LOST GENERATION

Have You Seen The Fallen?
Where They Lay,
One on One,
Across Your Somme,
Where They Fell,
One on One,
Upon The Wire,
Where The Poppies Grow,
One On One,
Crimson with Blood,
    Spilt For Thee,

Marking,
That Lost Generation,
Having Taken The Shilling!!

                  The Youth Of The Great War

BLACKPOOL

Blackpool Is A Bit Of A Carnival-Weird Place,
Dominated By The Its Tower,
Like The Roller Coaster,
Folks Are Always Clowning Around,
                                      Here,

People Are Certainly Not Themselves,
Beneath The Lights,
Its All False,
      Here,

With So Many Hens And Stags,
Rough Sleepers,
Lying In Doorways,
On Beds,
Huddled With Their Cardboard,
And Huddled Masses,

Then Of Course One Get The Holiday Makers,
That Drift Like Ships In The Night,
For No One Is Themselves Here,

What With Candy Floss 'n' Ices,
 Not Forgetting Those Awful Kiss Me Quick Hats,

304

Sold By The Dozen,
For If You And Want A Bit Of Peace,
I Wouldn't Choose Blackpool?

COMMODORE LADY

Commodore Lady,
I Remember Well.
Shrouded In Trees,
With Dogs A-Barking,
And A Lonely Figure,
Standing,
We Thought He Was A Bit Strange?
We Did As Kids,
My Commodore Lady,

Then A Knew Family Moved In,
Chopping Those Ole Cedar Down,
Lifting Your Veil,
Oh Commodore Lady,
That You May Have Sight To See,
Both Lundy High Bound To Be Dry,
And Old Taw Mouth,
And Its Lapping Waters,

You Commodore Lady,
With Boats And Buoys,
Who Pays The Ferryman?
For The Sands Are Running,
Beware You Don't Get Caught Out?

So Fair Commodore Lady!!

        Dedicated To The Woolaway Family
                                      Instow

ESTUARY VIEWS

Estuary Views Are Grand Here,
For It's Just Another Day In Paradise,
Smell The Salt Sea Airs,
When Skies Are Blue,
Or Perhaps Its Herringbone?
When I'm On The Balcony,
Having My Mug Of Rosie Lee,
After Picking Up Flotsam And a Jetsam,
                    On The Tide Line,

For One Can Hear The Yard,
Down Stream-Aways,
Echoing,
Rippling,
On The Tide Line,
As Both Dogs And Children Play,

When Sail Boats Pass,
Rasing,
Tacking,
In The Local Regatta,
For Who Pays Te Ferryman,
When The Ferry Doesn't Run?
You Can Certainly Hear The Bells Of Taw Mouth,

                              Ring Out,

For Old Taw Mouth Has Stood Guard,
Watching,
Just Watching,
Gazing Seaward,
Over These Fine Devon Estuary Views.

                    Afternoon Tea At The Commodore
                                             Instow

DIANA

Diana,

Our Queen Of Hearts,
With Both Lovers At Will,
The Huntress,
And The Hunted,
Dying In A Tunnel,
Black As Sins,
For It Was Foreign Soil,
Named After A Greek Warrior,
                              Pairs,

Oh Pairs,
My Gay Pairs,
She Took That Journey,
In To Deaths Dark Veil,

And The Seine Cried Tears,
With The People,
For Their Queen Of Hearts!

                                  Diana R.T.A.
                                  31 August 1997

BIGLINS
(Desecration Of A Quaint Old Cornish Town)

Empty Was The Old Place,
Up For Sale,
Was Biglins,

For It Had Been A Fisherman's Cottage,
But Alas No More,
Just Like Others,
It To Stood Empty,
And Up For Grabs,

For The Fishermen Are Told They Can't Fish For Pollock,
Therefore There Is No Fishin',
No Pollock, No Jobs,

And So With Grim Faces,
The Fishermen Are Resigned To Sell Their Boats,
And So Then Their Homes Go Up For Sale,
For A Pretty Penny,
               Like Old Biglins,

Then The Gulls Cry,
Around The Harbour,

Of This Quaint Old Cornish Town,
For Different Voices Are Heard Between The Lanes,
Strange Voices Moving In,
New Comers,
With A Pretty Penny Or Two,

Only Then To Rent Out,
Sadly To Those They Know,
And To Those They Don't,
Making More Pretty Pennies,
During Lighter Days Of The Season,
Whilst The Sun Is Hot,
For A Pretty Penny Or Two,

And So That Leaves both Harbour 'n' Lanes,
Lookin' Like A Wretched Ghost Town,
For The Nine Long Hard Months,
Of Winter,

What With The Winds Rattling,
Up Those Lanes.
Even For Blowin' Those Bins Over,
A Long The London Road!!

        Dedicated To The Fishing Folk Of The UK

B-IS 4 BLOSSOM

Blossoms Drift Past My Window,
                        Just So,

More In Hope,
Covering Our Little Red Mini,

Lookin' Like Flakes Of Snow,
Virgin White Snow,

        You Know!!

THE OLD CANAL

Murky,
Was The Old Canal,
For I Recall It Well,
It Was Used Then,
As Nothing More Than A Dumping Ground,
With Supermarket Trollies,
Prams And The Like,
You Can See The Kind Of Picture,
           I Am Recalling,

Whilst Under The Old Bridge,
The Kids Smoked Dope,
And Kissed And That,
For Yes Condoms Were Found,
You Might Of Said,
That It Was A Experimental Zone?
What With The Dirty Ole Tunnel Of Love,

What With Its History,
Of Dirty Old Sooty Ole Barges,
Black And Stained,
For It Was As Black As An Old Top Hat,
That's Why I'm Leaving It Now,
           With My Memories!

MENTAL HEALTH
(Nearing The End)

A Large Black Cloud It Hangs,
Although The Skies Are Blue,

Swifts They Dart,
A Farmer Crouches Over The Wheel,

Alone With His Thought,
Driving The Tractor,

Depressed,
Ploughing,

Ploughing On,
His Lonely Furrow,

Wearing A Mask,
Trying To Find His Way!

THE DAY AFTER

The Day After Tomorrow,
Looms Over Us!

THE DIAGNOSIS

Have You Had A Diagnosis?
For When You Have A Diagnosis,
It Hits You In The Solar Plexus,
Up Turning Lives,
And All Who Know You?
For Yes The World Might Seem More Alive?
The Skies May Seem Bluer?
For The Grass Could Even Seem Green?
What With The Breezes A-Buzzin'?
And The Birds A-Nesting,
Especially If It Is Spring Time,
For When It Is Autumn,
One Has The Colours,
It Is Then One Realises The World Is A Beautiful Place,
With It Lakes And Mountains,
Coast And River Estuaries,
There For Shout To Your God,
And Shout For Joy!!

MINORITIES

We All Minorities,
Now Folks,

The Christian,
The Muslim,
The Jew,
The Sikh,
The Hindu,
The L.G.B.T.
The Disabled,

For We're All In This Stew Pot,
                      Together,

Like A Many Layered Onion!!

                                  The UK To Day

FOR THIS IS ALL I KNOW

Oh I am Not Disabled,
For This Is All I Know,
      You Know,

The Disability Comes From Yourselves,
In What You Think,
In How You Re-Act,
      You Know,

And Please Don't Stare,
Or Pity,
For Know One Likes That,
      You Know,

And Please Remember Disability,
Could Walk Its Ugly Way?
To You,
      You Know!

NUMBER 9

Venus,

She Stepped Out Of Her Shell,
With A Hello Guys,
I'm Yours,
Your Mine,
This Rounded,
Curved Woman Of Mine,
Stating To Me,
At Number 9,
For We'll Say No More,
Though Please Remember,
The Number Is,
Number 9,

And I Could Feel My Halo Slipping,
At The Door Of Number 9!!

ON THE ELEVENTH DAY

On The Eleventh Day,
Of The Eleventh Hour,
At The Eleventh Month,
The King He Leads The Nation,
With Wreaths 'n' Poppies,
In Remembering,
Those Who Have Been Killed Or Wounded
                              In Action,

So That We May Live In Our Today,
As Well As Their Tomorrow!

EASTER DAY

When All Things Seem Lost,
There Is Easter Day!!!!

THE BOAT RACE

Oxford Blue,

Cambridge Blue,

On A Tidal River,

Through A Capital City,

With Their Ores,

A-Wash,

Busy Stroking,

From Putney,

To Mortlake.

PUBLIC LIMITED COMPANY

The UK P.L.C.
Is Like A Many Layered Onion,

Therefore Friend,

Don't Be COLOUR BLIND!

ENCOUNTER

Even With Closed Eye,
I Spied It Well,
In All Grace,
Majesty,
And Triumphant,
I Did Happen To Stumble Over,
The Great White Stag,
Shrouded By The Forest Trees,
                        Dark,

And The Light Had No Purpose,
Deep With On The Forest Floor,
For The Great White Stag,
Had Become The Light,
As The Eagle Soared High,
With His Revelation,
And So The Creatures Of The Forest Floor,
Did Come Like I,
And Did Worship,
The Great White Stag,
Of The Early Celtic Saints,

Who Did They Erect And Worship, Churches And
Standing Stones,

Whence First Meeting With The Great White Stag,
Of The Forest Floor,

For Then At Once We Saw A Blackened Abode Lurking,
For It Was The Smoulderin' Wizard Of Ills,
Ready To Snarl With Hate,
For Some Of The Little Creatures Were Afraid,
And Had Labelled Him Either The Red Dragon,
Or All Hallows Witch,
Although I To Knew Did Finally Know He Was Defeated,
For I Had Been Summand Through My Journey,
Now Only To Arrive Here At The Great White Stags Calling!!!

ODE TO NICK

I saw him Marry,

I saw him grow,

I saw his Daughter,

I saw him Fly,

I saw him Crash,

For the Argentine blew Him out of the Sky,

There by taking His Life,

And then Mrs. 'T'

Order the sinking of the "Belgrano"

Flight Lieutenant Nick Taylor
Died Falklands, 1982 - Friend
Falklands Remembered 1982 - 2022

NICK'S SOLITARY DAUGHTER

Oh I Am Nick's Solitary Daughter,
For I Don't Remember,
My Loving Father,
For I Was But Eighteen Months,
When He Left Us,
Sailing On The South Atlantic Fleet,
To Fly,
Most Of Us,
Hardly Knew God Knows Where,

To Meet His Death,
So Sudden,
Shot Down On That Foreign Soil,
Like They Did,
Was A Cruel Thing To Happen,
To A Sailor Boy,

An' So We Recall,
My Dad,
The Flying Sailor Boy,
In These Photo's,
Now,
For They Are But Few,
For Tell Me More Of Him,

You-The Poet!

Flt Lieutenant Nick Taylor Remembered

OUR RECLUSE

With Hand Bag Like The Queen,
The Woman On Her Own,
She Has Locked Herself Away,
No More Does She Answer The Phone,
Neither Go Out On Her Own,
Wearing That Disarming Smile,
      What's The Story?

Behind The Mask,
Of Course Covid Didn't Help,
Living Alone,
For God I Trust She Does Not,
Hit The Flowing Waters Of Life,
Though Once I am Told,
She Travelled Widely,

But Not Anymore,
What Happened To Our Recluse?
What's The Story?
For There Has To Be More,
Our Line To Take,

As This Softly Spoken Genteel Sort,
With Draws From The World,

Hiding,
The Life She Has To Given,
With A Treasure Of Boxes,
All Secrets,
Covert Like,
For Our Recluse Is Always Interested In You?
Although Never Divulging Herself,
Then Who Is She?
Our Recluse,
Kind Awkward In Mind And Walk,
Not Letting This World In,
      Just So Close!!

PATTERNS OF FAITH

The Notations Of Our Streets,
Are All At Once Hand Bags,
And Glad Bags,
With Sounds Of Sally Army Bands,
At Christmas Time,
In Tills Of Tinsel 'N' Glitter,
When Listening For The Sounds,
Of Christmas Choral Ayrs,

Wandering Through Ones Ears,
In Patterns Of Faith,
For The Waters Are Flowing Black,
Deep,
When Now Staining Of Men,
Looking,
Learning On,
When Teaching The Babe,
To Watch,
Among Wrapping Unfolding,
        To Years!!!

                      Xmas 24

THE NOTION OF OUR SEAS

Have You Heard The Notion Of Our Seas?
Through Ones Ears,
Told Upon The Mantles Shell,
When Lapping The Sands,
Gently So One Kisses Our Shore,
Carryin' Trash Of Men's Desire,
For Our Septic Isle,
When Told,
For We Are A Travellin' Kind,
Visitin' Other Shores-A-Far,
On Wing Of Bird 'N' Fortunes Weather,
When Catchin' The Light,
As Well As Fish,
For Now Kernow's Old Wheel Houses Fall To Ruin 'N' Why?
You Left Ones Tin And Your Chips,
Once Then With Compass Wide,
For Our Tides Of Blue Is Turning When,
So Listen 'N' Paint The Picture Well,
Knowin' The Rocks Are Sharpe,
When Espying Dolphin And Mermaids Play!!

Falmouth, Cornwall
2024

THE AIR RAID
(The White Poppy)

When Both Mother And Son,
      On Sirens Wail,

Heard A Most Fearful Sound,
For What Was To Come,
And Yet Mother Prayed,
Knowing Her Son Already Lost His Father,
Though Still They Fell Like Rain,
           Black Rain,

To Bomb And To Destroy,
Towns And Lives A-Ruin,
War Was No longer At The Front,

For You Have No Home,
No House In Which To Go,
When Emerging From The Shelter,
For Dodding's Big Wing Had Done Its Job!

THE WORST OF DAY

Oh Twenty Twelve,
Was Indeed My Worst Of Day,
For I Did Meet A Witch,
Then One Day,
Cursed So Was She,
That Woman Hurled Her Bag At Me,
For Breaking My Ribs,

And So Setting Up An Infection There,
In My Lung,
For Much Pain I Felt,
Taking Me Off My Legs,
There In The Hospital Bed,
To Ache,
I Had Them Pump,
By Medic's All,
For I Was On Oxen Then,

Raising An Eye To Heaven,
When Father Came,
The Angels Holy,
Did Recover Me,
During Three Long Years,
Leaving Me Tired Of This Lives Worries,

And Woes!

To Father Philip Of Ilfracombe

MOORLAND JAPS

It Came Upon Me,
Then One Day,
Whilst I Was Spirited Away,
On A Carpet Of Purple 'N' Song,
Did Those Crossing Ribbons Flow,

For Then I spied Old Daw,
Ridding His Chestnut Mare,
Tall In The Saddle Like,
Though Round And Fat Was He,
                              Old Daw,

For I Was Tall,
Although Still Small,
In The World I Saw,
Of Uncles And Aunts,
And Their Good Friends Then,
When Hunting On Those Moors,

Somewhat Green,
They Lead Me Like The Pipe-per,
Musical Norman And His Gang Of Old
Confederate Friends,

There Was Stick Jaw, Mountain, Hugging and Old Daw,
Not Forgetting Dear Lionel Shepherd Of His Sheep,

For The Japs they Did Play,
And Get Up Too,
Up That Moor Which Was Their Playground, Then,
Just As If They Were Boys,
For Once I Had Heard that The Fore mentioned Group
Of Confederate Friends Lead Old Mathews The Rector A -Stray,

The Rector Looked like Bloody Shakespeare,
And Thought He Was-In Something Of A Play
And So The Fore Mentioned Lead Him A -Stray,
One Christmas Eve,
With Ole Mary Janes Help,
Down At The Pub,
For Mathews Always Thought He Knew More Than They,
The Chap Was Red Faced For Weeks,
Poor Old Rector

And Then One Of Them Put A Sheet Over His Head,
Dragging A Chain Behind Him,
One Hallows Eve,
Through The Village,
           Then,

Only To Be Seen Sometime Later,
Leaving The Pub Jar In Hand,
Laughin' And Giggling Like Drains in The Rains,

Oh For I Could Tell You Oh So Many More Tales,
Of Those Moors,
Perhaps Another Day?

But For Now I'll Stop There,
For I Feel Old and Grown,
Not Young Anymore,
And Those Spirits Well They Have Flown!!!

                              To Father Fry

DANDELION MAN

When The Dandelion Man Spoke,
And Fire Flies Fly,
Fairies Come Out To Dance, The Night Away,

With Enchantment Song,
The Tides Are High,
And The Moon Comes Up,
Only To Say Goodbye,
Then It Is A Most Magical Night,
For Those Born With Flowers In Their Hair,

To Speak With The Dandelion Man,
Who Had Lost His Crown,
For Clother Was He,
When He Grinned At The Moon,
In A Birthday Suit As Never Before,

Do Nothing But Living On Jelly Beans,
And Coffee Creams,
Only To Ask Why?
To The Great Bear In The Sky,
On A Carpet Of Purple,
Smelling Of Roses,
And Rainbow Juice!!

Printed in Great Britain
by Amazon